TELLING
*the*TRUTH

Growing Up to Intimacy and Freedom

TELLING
*the*TRUTH

Growing Up to Intimacy and Freedom

by Brad Blanton, PhD.

SPARROWHAWK PUBLICATIONS

Stanley, Virginia

A Sparrowhawk Publications book
Stanley, Virginia

Designed by Donna Sicklesmith Anderson
Illustrations by Whitney Sherman
Printed by BookCrafters, Inc.
Manufactured in the United States of America

1 2 3 4 5 6 7 8 9 10

Library of Congress Cataloging-in-Publication Data
Blanton, Brad, 1991
    Telling the Truth
    1. Life 2. Success 3. Self-actualization I. Title

ISBN 0-963-09210-3

Dedicated to my Clients – Past, Present & Future

About the Author

Brad Blanton received his Ph.D. from the University of Texas in 1966. He was trained in Gestalt Therapy by Fritz Perls, M.D., Ph.D., the founder of Gestalt Therapy; Jim Simkin, Ph.D.; Robert Hall, M.D.; and many others central to the establishment of Gestalt Therapy in the United States. He was trained in hypnosis by Milton Erikson, M.D.

Dr. Blanton was founding President of the Gestalt Institute of Washington, D.C., in 1971, and started the first training program in Gestalt Therapy in the Washington D.C. area. He has been in the private practice of Clinical Psychology in Washington, D.C., for the past 20 years, and specializes in individual, group, and couples psychotherapy.

Dr. Blanton has been a participant in the Arica 40-Day training, est, Lifespring, Introduction to Neurolinguistic Programming, Rational Emotive Psychotherapy, the Communication Workshop, Werner Erhard & Associates' The Forum, The 6 Day, The Communication Course, Mastery of Empowerment trainings, and many other trainings. He has studied Yoga, Zen Buddhism, Transcendental Meditation, and various other meditation and self-defense systems under a variety of teachers. He studied Sufi drumming, exercise and dervish dancing under the Sufi teacher Adnan Sarhan.

In 1977, Dr. Blanton founded the Stress Management Science Institute to train members of the helping professions in psychotherapy and stress management techniques. In 1985 he established the Center for Well Being as a part of the outreach program of the Institute. He has taught, been a consultant, and conducted trainings in more than 40 local institutions and government agencies. Dr. Blanton is currently the director of the Center for Well Being, in Washington, D.C. and Sparrowhawk Farm in the Shenandoah Valley of Virginia, where he conducts the *Telling the Truth Nine Day Workshop*. He continues private practice. ⤙

Contents

Part Four:
THINGS LEARNED FROM THE WAR BETWEEN BEING & MIND

Acknowledgments

I have had a lot of help writing this book. So many people have given me help over the last six years, I'm sure to leave some of them out. At the top of the list, the one who has cared the most, edited the most, argued the most, and helped write the most is Amy Silverman, who did all that while still performing a great number of other nurturing and supportive services beyond the call of normal wifely duty during the same time period. Thank you Amy. You are the wind beneath my wings.

Grace Tiffany, Mike Snell, Michael Zuckerman, Susan Kelly, Betsy Perkins, Mary Harrill, Jane Ashley, Donna Sicklesmith, Frank Sokolof, Sondra Zahn-Oreck, Michael Lamas and Sandy Ross all helped edit large parts of the book and gave me feedback, assistance, support and instruction in writing. Thank you. I appreciate you all for helping me. I couldn't have done it without you.

Many thanks also to Heather Schoen and Clyde McElvene for help in pulling the book together and helping me begin to present the book and the ideas therein to the general public. Many creative thanks to Paul Fetters, Jay Sumner, Whitney Sherman and Donna Sicklesmith (again) for photographing, illustrating and designing the book. Thanks to Lolinda Moseley for the work you did at the Library of Congress. Thanks to Carolyn Meyer who helped pull the bibliography together and write letters requesting permission to use the quotes from all the people I quoted, and helped with the mailing list for the book signing party. Thanks to the members of my Mastery of Empowerment Group: Ed Greville, Pam and Kent Cartwright, Clyde McElvene, Roger Johnson, Michael Fogarty, Paul Fetters, Jay Sumner, and Marcia Makepeace for all of your early support and ongoing support and feedback during this whole process. Thanks to all of my friends who bought advance copies to help me pay for publishing this book. My individual acknowledgments of you are handwritten here at the bottom of this page. If this becomes a financial success I'll give you all your money back and some free copies to hand out to friends.

So many of you did extra things you didn't have to do, things sometimes I didn't even know I needed, and I appreciate you all so much for taking care of me in my ignorance and making me more capable than I really am. To whatever degree this book is a contribution to other people, your help and support made that contribution possible.

—WBB

Publisher's Preface

THIS BOOK is not worth publishing.

I submitted the manuscript of this book to many agents and publishers. It was accepted for representation and publication several times under the condition that they could tell me how to rewrite it, they would have all of the power to say what was in it, and they would keep most of the money made from it. From their point of view, I was lucky they would even consider taking me on to straighten me out. This book doesn't meet the standards of the publishing industry. As many agents and publishers have told me, this book is flawed. I quote too many people and the quotes are too long. I mix literature with essay. I should decide whether I am writing a psychological self-help book or a socio-political commentary — they are two different things. I say bullshit, they are not. They are intimately related.

Nevertheless, I am really grateful to the agents, editors and friends that have taught me so much about writing these past five years. I spent almost two years writing proposals for publishing companies in which I had to say what this book was about, and it helped me enormously. It also helped me get clear about who I am and what I have to say and how I want to say it differently than I am supposed to.

This book is a hodgepodge of historical sociological essay, adventure stories, personal stories, advice-column advice, how-to-do it manual, poetry, and psychological theory and practice. This is a self-help book for a world of human beings who are on the brink of destruction or rebirth.

There is not only something wrong with the book, there is something wrong with me. I cuss too much. I am unprofessional both as a psychotherapist and as a writer. I am an anti-moralism moralist and I write righteously indignant diatribes against righteous indignation. I contradict myself. I have great ideas and a lot to say, but I'm not much of a writer. I don't learn to control myself and do what is required.

Unfortunately or fortunately, this mess is the heart of what I have to offer to the world. I'm really a kind of pathetic person, careening down the road of life, battered between pillar and post, bouncing from "God knows I'm sorry," to "Fuck 'em if they can't take a joke." I was a lower class boy who made it big in the middle class world. I am not impressed with either one of those provincial states of mind. I don't have much respect for other cultures either. Bullshit abounds everywhere the world over as far as I can tell. When I am in Rome I do not want to do as the God-damned Romans do because they are just as fucked up as I am, or worse. The same for anywhere else and the same for the publishing industry.

I am good at mixing worlds and then unmixing them again, but differently. I love learning, even though I am a slob about it. I consume information from many sources. I keep what seems to be nourishing and life-sustaining and useful from conversations with people, spit out what I can't use, and share whatever I come up with in other conversations with other people.

I am a translator across barriers of feeling and thought. I am a transliterator of meaning from one language to another, from sub-culture to sub-culture, culture to culture, eastern world to western world. I appreciate the hell out of anything written or told to me that works for me in my life.

I am inordinately interested in the truth, which I am able to tell is true by how it works in my life. I don't give a shit about form or about formulas that are merely traditional. I am not impressed with the argument that unity of form maximizes communication, nor that it is what causes books to sell.

So I am publishing this God-damned thing myself. Fuck 'em if they can't take a joke. If you are standing in the store reading this, and you don't want to buy it, put the sonofabitch down so somebody who might buy it can pick it up and look at it. ᐁ

— *Brad Blanton*
SPARROWHAWK PUBLICATIONS, July 1991

Introduction

I am fifty years old. I have been a psychotherapist in Washington, D.C., for 20 years. People come to my office and pay me money to pay attention to them and do what I can to help out. I have some skill in helping people find ways to make their lives work. This is what I have learned:

We all lie like hell. It wears us out. It is *the* major source of all human stress. Lying kills people.

The kind of lying that is most deadly is withholding, or keeping back information from someone we think would be affected by it. Psychological illness of the severest kind is the result of this kind of lying. Psychological healing is possible only with the freedom that comes from not hiding anymore. Keeping secrets and hiding from other people is a trap. Adolescents spend most of their time playing this hide-and-seek game. The better you are at getting by with playing hide-and-seek during adolescence, the harder it is to grow up. "Important" secrets and all the plotting and cogitation that go with them are all bullshit.

The mind is a jail built out of bullshit. This book tells how the bullshit jail of the mind gets built and how to escape. This is a "how to" book on freedom. Withholding from other people, not telling them about what we feel or think, keeps us locked in the jail. The longer we remain in that jail, the quicker we decline. We either escape, or we go dead. The way out is to get good at telling the truth.

My clients are mostly people in the 20- to 50-year age range who are depressed, anxious, angry, burnt out, or a combination thereof. I work with government employees, lawyers, business people, media professionals, and other overgrown adolescents with super-critical minds who can't stop judging and criticizing themselves and moralizing to other people. I work to relieve their suffering, primarily the suffering of deadness. Deadness is a low-intensity form of suffering. It is the result of staying on guard against imagined greater dangers. The greater dangers we imagine are based on memories of how we have been hurt before. Many of us learned as children that being fully alive was bad and you got hurt for it, so we deadened ourselves: partly as a defense against the big people, and partly to spite them. Deadening ourselves was our way of hiding that we were alive in improper ways, and the only thing to do was to keep it a secret.

The path we must follow to get over the suffering of deadness leads, initially, into greater suffering. For example, if you have deadened yourself for a long time to keep from experiencing anger, getting very angry will feel worse than deadness. But it's only your willingness to feel worse that will allow you to feel better. Trying to remain carefully kept and avoid further pain, embarrassment and difficulty is normal. Normality is the key to avoiding change and continuing to suffer. People who want to be normal are often proud of it and victims to the ideal of normality: dead-suffering, death-dealing normality. Sigmund Freud once said that psychoanalysis was to help people get from intense suffering to common unhappiness. I don't think we have to settle for that. I help people focus their attention and muster their courage for the journey into previously avoided suffering, and then beyond to a truly abnormal life. Facing what one has previously avoided results in intense emotion and then a breakthrough into overflowing creativity. That overflowing creativity is the source of power for changing or re-shaping our lives.

I work like a body-shop mechanic works to fix a bent fender. When, how, and particularly *why* an accident occurred doesn't make a damn bit of difference to a body-shop man. He's only interested in results. He'll bang around the outside of the fender with a rubber mallet, tap it from the inside with a ball peen hammer, drill a hole, attach a rod, and try to pull it out or hit it with a rock. When it pops out, if it does, he sands it off, paints it and sends it out. If it doesn't pop out, he replaces it. He is pragmatic, experienced, and confident of the essential flexibility of the material with which he works. Careful attention to detail and experimentation with each new dent brings consistent results.

I work on individual, self-created suffering with people who are responsible for continuing to create their own suffering. Like the body-shop man and the owner of the car, we concentrate on the condition of the machine and the results we want; we don't have to figure out how the accident happened, and we judge the success or failure of our efforts by how close we've come to the results we want.

I work mostly with "garden variety" neurotics: average, basically healthy people who are anxious or depressed or both. Often these general states of being — anxiety or depression — are accompanied by somatic discomforts and diseases such as skin rashes, ulcers, lower back pain, spastic colitis, allergies, high blood pressure, and insomnia; or by recurring problems in relationships, on the job, or in the family. When therapy works, the somatic ills disappear or decrease in intensity; anxiety and depression as steady states go away; and people take responsibility for making their relationships, professional lives, and creative powers work. Taking *responsibility* means a person no longer blames outside circumstances, or other people, or past events for the conditions of his own life.

Both the bodily ills and the steady unwanted emotional states go away because of a learning that takes place, and that learning always involves letting up on the demand that the world, including the demander, be other than what it *is*. Therapy is over when a person stops incessantly demanding that other people be different from what they are, forgives his or her parents and other begrudged former intimates, re-claims the power to make life work, and takes responsibility for doing so.

Psychotherapy doesn't always work. My estimate is that about a third of the time the results are good to adequate, about a third of the clients make a few half-assed changes, and at least a third of the folks who see me don't get any good out of therapy worth mentioning. Very few people suffer any damage in therapy since it is as hard to do damage as it is to help. I have seen a lot of failure and a lot of success. This book is an attempt to say what works, when it works. When therapy works, the result is an experience of well being, wholeness, being whole. This book is about getting there.

Where Does Stress Come From?

People say modern life is stressful. Stress is not a characteristic of life or times, but of people. Stress does not come from the environment, it comes from the mind of the individual under stress. We make certain assumptions about the world, and we become attached to those assumptions. We suffer from thinking. We worked too hard to learn our ideas about the world to give them up. Like poker players who have already lost too much, we desperately double the bet in hopes of forcing fate to give us a good card. We think about things too much and too seriously and we suffer a great deal from trying to make the world match our thinking. We complain about how the world fails to live up to our expectations. We think about how life doesn't live up to its billing, and how it should, and how it is rotten that it doesn't, and how we should somehow fix it. Many people think themselves to death.

In order to survive, we have to apply what we have learned from experience. But it is equally true that in order to thrive — in order to stay alive — we have to *overcome* continually what we have previously learned. If we don't somehow get rescued from our assumptions about life, they devour us. Rescue involves recognizing that the assumptions we so stubbornly cling to as truths are, in fact, decisions we have made about what "should be true" based on past experiences.

The Truth Changes

Because of being lost in our own minds, we fail to recognize that the truth changes. When the truth changes and we fail to recognize what has *now* become true, while holding on to the *idea* of what used to be true, we become liars committing suicide. If at 8:00 pm, I am mad at you and tell you about it and get quite worked up over it, and you get mad back and we talk about it, and we stay committed to the conversation and to the possibility of getting over our anger, there is a good chance that by 8:45 pm we can laugh and have a drink and not be angry anymore. It was true that I hated your guts at 8:00 pm. It was no longer true somewhere between 8:20 and 8:45. In contrast, people who live according to principles, like "I hated you then, and for good reason, so I still hate you now," can't get over things. This is reasonable but stupid. I have seen a lot of reasonably stupid people in my life.

Life goes on, and the truth changes; this just happens to be the way life is. What was once true is often no longer true just a little while later. Yesterday's truth is today's bullshit. Even yesterday's liberating insight is today's jail of stale explanation.

Roles and rules are also thoughts, which, when grasped onto as principles, are hard for people to get over, or get beyond or let change. People choke the life out of themselves by tying themselves to a chosen "self image" — any "self image" whatsoever. Many adults remain in a perpetual adolescence, locked in the protective confinement of a limited set of roles and rules. This protection kills. According to a study conducted by The Centers for Disease Control in Atlanta, 53% of the people who die prior to age 65 do so "for reasons directly related to lifestyle."[1] Half of the people who die earlier than expected kill themselves by how they live. I say they kill themselves compensating for the starvation of being cut off from the nourishment of commonplace experience. They smoke, drink, take drugs, eat fat meat, watch TV, and don't exercise. They work hard to survive and take care of themselves and their families. They try to have a good time and do the best they can. They are constantly doing the best they can and not having it be good enough. They kill themselves with the same socially acceptable poisons all their friends use. They all were very much in touch with being alive at one time and then got more and more lost in their minds. They miss something they can't quite get back to. They know a renewed love of life has something to do with escaping their own minds and the conditions of life their minds have set up, but they just can't seem to do so. Moralism, a disease of living in the mind without relief, kills them. They die, trapped in some country song, doing the best they can and trying to have a little fun, but never doing well enough to suit anybody, particularly themselves, or having enough fun to make up for the strain.

Freedom from such a "life" is a psychological achievement. The freedom achieved by people who grow beyond the limitations of their childhood conditioning is freedom from their own minds. Freedom *from* one's own mind is freedom *to* create. But in order to have some say in creating life, you must be willing to tell the truth. Telling the truth frees us from entrapment in the mind.

The alternative to freedom is to live out a program imposed

by prefabricated internalized moral resolves. Living this way is a gradual suffocation, which makes us simultaneously more dead and more desperate.

Creativity, *using* the mind rather than being used *by* the mind, is the cure for all stress disorders. Willingness to tell the truth in order to be free from your secretly assessing, secret-keeping mind creates the possibility of using your mind to make a future as an artist rather than as a victim.

Bullshit

Bullshit is a highly technical term used throughout this book. I stole this term from Fritz Perls, the father of Gestalt Therapy. Abstraction from past experience mistaken for current experience itself is the major disorienting mistake of the normal garden-variety neurotic. We neurotics are people who make big generalizations to cover long periods of time. We say things like, "You *always*..." and "You *never*...." We attribute all of our power to circumstances and say things like "*It* makes me...." When we say these things we usually have no idea we are living in an imaginary world of our own creation. Fritz Perls actually made three technical distinctions for poisonous assignment of value: chickenshit, bullshit, and elephant shit. Chickenshit is a normal greeting that doesn't mean what it says, as in "Hello, how are you?" "I'm fine, how are you?" Bullshit is normal conversation in which people are simply whiling away the time with meaningless abstractions and generalizations. Elephant shit is any discussion of Gestalt theory.

I use words that have "shit" in them to give a pejorative evaluation of evaluations themselves. I want people at least to consider the possibility that their most valuable values may not be so valuable. I want people to question their own certainty. (As Nietzsche said, "Not doubt, *certainty* is what drives one insane."[2]) So, for simplicity's sake, I will use "bullshit" as the generic root word for all value-assigned abstraction or summations of remembered experiences.

Bullshit is any abstraction from experience your mind makes and assigns value to. "You don't love me," or "Those people are angry," or "This is ugly (beautiful, good, bad, important, etc.)" all are *interpretations* of reality. Bullshit is a sales pitch for an interpretation of reality that comes with any interpretation of reality. *All* interpretations of reality are bullshit. Freedom is not being dominated by your own bullshit.

We believe our interpretations of reality intensely, and we want other people to join us in our interpretations to make us feel secure. We believe our interpretations *are* reality and if we can get enough votes we will prove it.

A few of us occasionally escape the bullshit jail of the mind. Most of us die in jail. All of us have the magnificent possibility of getting beyond the jail of our own minds, over and over again. The first step to this process is to doubt our minds. The truth turns to bullshit in the human mind just like food turns to shit in the human body. Our minds work pretty much the same way our gastrointestinal systems work. A mind is developed to take good nourishing truth, absorb what it can, and turn the rest to shit. Unfortunately, the mind doesn't expel shit automatically like the body does. We have to do it voluntarily.

According to Hugh Thomas, author of *A History of The World,* the greatest medical advance in history has been garbage collection.[3] The greatest psychological advance in history is just around the corner and will also have to do with cleaning up. Cleaning up lies and "coming out of the closet" is getting more attention these days. Some day we will look back on these years of suffocation in bullshit in the same way we look back on all the years people lived in, and died from, their garbage.

Lying

This book unfolds developmentally, beginning with an accounting of how a mind grows from nothing to what it is by the time it reaches adolescence. The central message of this book is that we human beings, in the course of growing up, get lost in our minds; and if we don't find our way out, our minds eventually kill us.

We all have minds, and we all come by them naturally. In learning how to survive from birth to adulthood, we start out using our *senses* as a primary mode of orientation in the world and we end up as minded beings using *principles* of orientation. We abstract from our senses and form our minds. After a while we get so involved in mind development that we lose touch with our senses and get lost in our minds. Our minds are formed of interpretations about reality based on replicated experiences. After a baby experiences being nursed repeatedly, it starts anticipating being nursed again based on hunger and its little memory, and it cries for more milk. When more milk comes quickly a tiny little concept involving time has been born. The baby has an interpretation: "If I cry, I'll get milk." That interpretation has a memory in it and an expectation for the future.

As we grow, we learn to interpret our experience in order to survive. We eventually become capable of caring for ourselves, but our survival techniques can, and often do, eventually kill us. What kills us is intense attachment to our interpretations and failure to distinguish these interpretations from sensate reality. This process of learning to categorize experiences, and then forgetting the distinction between categories and experience itself, is what I call learning how to lie.

Learning how to pretend, interpret, evaluate, and imagine is a natural process for every human being. It's fun. Most of the learning that occurs in early childhood, pre-school and elementary school is an elaboration of these abilities. In every culture of the world, as infants grow toward adulthood, this learning of pretense is going on.

The long process of learning how to lie culminates in adolescence. Adolescents get lost in their imaginings about who they are. Erik Erikson says that the question being asked during adolescence is, "Who am I?," and the answer eventually reached is either fragmentary (role confusion) or unified (ego identity)[4]. In order to mature beyond the role-playing or pretending stage, the question "Who am I?" must get answered in some unitary way (the numerous roles kids try on for size have to become integrated into a consistent identity that remains even when new roles are adopted). This uniquely synthesized personality eventually has to predominate over role requirements as demonstrated by role models, or by ideal role performance. There has to be a "Jillness" about the way Jill plays the role of daughter, lover, and waitress that is there all the time she is talking to her mother, being with her lover, or waiting tables. This "Jillness" stands out regardless of whether mother, lover, or customers are in the environment, and regardless of how she has seen the roles played on TV.

The duration of this developmental stage, the stage of pretending and trying on roles to establish or invent who you are, depends on the culture in which you live. The more technological the culture, the longer the stage endures. Bushmen have one year — from 11 to 12 years of age — to form their identities; by the age of 12 they have chosen a vocation, gotten married, started making babies, and assumed adult roles. In our culture, adolescence lasts from age 11 to about 30 or 35.

This extension of the time to choose vocational, sexual, and social identities in highly technological cultures is a mixed bag. *Right now the fastest growing death rate in our society is for people between the ages of 15 and 24.* Suicides, drug overdoses, and accidents head the list of causes. We get a longer time to invent who we are, but the job takes a greater toll.

Even when people survive the years of adolescence, the great majority never get over the pretense of adolescence. Enormous suffering is caused by being lost in such pretense. Frequently, "helping professionals" recommend more pretending or more conventional pretending, because they don't understand that the job of psychotherapy is to re-ground people in the world of experience.

The stress that kills or cripples most of the population comes from people being too hard on themselves when they don't live up to their own imaginings about how other people think they should behave. We don't know who we are, and we try to guess who we ought to be in order to do the right thing and be happy. We get lost in the process and beat the hell out of ourselves before we even know we're hurt. It does no good whatsoever simply to change what we imagine others expect of us. We need to recover the ability to pay attention to something other than the whirlpool of questions and doubts about what is required or expected for acceptance. We have lost this ability to pay attention — to live outside the set of assumptions a mind is — and the only method of orientation left is given by the roles we have been trying on for size. Thus, we run around in the world while running around in our minds trying to live up to standards we imagine others are requiring of us, while we starve for the nourishment that comes from commonplace experience. We end up trying to eat the menu instead of the meal. Menus are nutritionally without value and taste like shit no matter what pretty pictures decorate their surface.

Adolescents miss the security of childhood and can't stand the uncertainty of being between childhood and adulthood. Out of anxiety and intolerance for ambiguity they grasp onto roles or rigid standards to claim an identity so they can escape the interminable struggle over how to fit in. They become Christians or Hari Krishnas or gang members or hippies, or marry a childhood sweetheart, just to have a place to stand. They adopt the standards and principles of these groups to live by. Standards or principles to live by *are all equal in this way: they are abstractions of the mind, summations based on past experience, not experience itself.*

Adolescents of all ages become more passionately attached to standards the more insecure they feel. Strong attachment to principle only increases our rigidity, which further increases our feeling of insecurity. Such behavior doesn't guide us through our changing experiences. The world of experience is like a river. You are better off with a boat than with a post to hold on to while the water beats you to death.* To grow beyond adolescence, people have to let go of, rather than tighten their grip on, the principles and standards with which they define themselves. This is usually very scary, like falling backward into the unknown. What results is experience in the here and now. The re-emergence of this struggle, the struggle for identity that was put away by grasping onto an identity out of an intolerance of ambiguity, is the most valuable function of psychotherapy for people who are frozen in role definitions. These people are reborn from their mental jail into the here and now.

Such people learn to treat principles, not as rules engraved in stone, but as less important "rules of thumb" to be validated or invalidated by new experience. Rules of thumb can be revised or rejected or created anew if the people who hold them make allowances to include new experience. People who are intensely attached to moral principles notice only the experiences that justify the rightness of the principles and simply don't notice anything else.

Fritz Perls, one of my teachers, recommended that people "lose their minds and come to their senses." Unless people who have grown minds learn to lose their minds and come to their

---

*Alan Watts' book, *The Wisdom of Insecurity*, is an elaboration of this point.

senses again — pay attention to gravity, their own bodies, the world of real objects and other beings out there — they remain locked in their own tightly held notions of "how things are" and never notice any new experiences. Yogis, Buddhist monks, golf pros, a few psychotherapy clients, some musicians, and an odd assortment of others *regain* their ability to pay attention in spite of the minds they have developed. These people somehow progress beyond being trapped in and dominated by the "mindstream," to the exclusion of everything else.

A mind is a terrible thing; waste it.

This book delineates the problems that result from *not* escaping your constantly interpreting, lying mind; of *not* growing beyond the developmental stage of learning how to lie. It gives examples of how withholding the truth from other people kills or gravely dampens the life of the withholder.

Psychotherapy is one way of learning how to finish growing up: how to get to creativity from the intermediate developmental stage of adolescent lying and fantasizing. What I have developed is a treatment for the problem of being stuck in adolescence, a problem I believe is shared by more than 75 per cent of the population of the modern technological world. The essential treatment method is a clear intention, agreed upon between therapist and client together, to tell the truth to each other and to everyone else the client knows personally, in order to find our way out of the maze. This holds the great promise of bringing us to a more adult way of living — grounded in experience, less superstitious, and less moralistic. Ironically, to mature fully, we must rediscover what we knew when we were less sophisticated. Once we have re-centered ourselves in our experience, which is the position we inhabited as children, we can finally use our minds as instruments for creation rather than as defense systems for our image of who we are.

Ultimately, we can unite the real world of experience in the here and now with the world we "know about" from memory and interpretation. The secret of this union is to release energy by living out loud rather than spending all of our energy trying to control ourselves and others through withholding. The secret, in other words, is telling the truth. Growth into the personal power of telling the truth is the key to life beyond adolescent moralism.

Psychotherapy is one method of rescue from being choked to death by concepts which were learned for the sake of efficiency and to avoid unwanted experience. As I said, sometimes it works and sometimes it doesn't. *The effectiveness of psychotherapy depends entirely on the client's commitment to telling the truth and this applies to the client's behavior inside and outside the therapy room.*

There are many ancient systems of thought dealing with the stages of growth beyond lying and posing. Most historical spiritual/religious/mythological teachings are based on the psychological growth of a few wise people who marked out a path for others to follow. In our age, the opportunity has come for all of us to learn the whole path.

If we humans are to be saved from ourselves, individually as well as collectively, we have to learn more about the art and science of speaking the truth. None of us can do it without a lot of help from each other.

Summary

My clients and I have been learning from each other that the primary requirement for getting beyond adolescence is telling the truth. This book deals with the whole problem of telling the truth: the difficulty in telling the truth, how it hurts one not to tell the truth, how we are all liars, and how it works against our self-interest to lie. It is common for people to ruin their lives and kill themselves through withholding. It is normal for people to stop growing and die from an accumulation of mild stress disorders over time. Being overweight, uptight, a heavy smoker, a heavy drinker, a non-exerciser, or some combination thereof, are the direct result of a more central ailment of the mind. These deaths come from remaining enmeshed in the mind — trapped in lies. Escape from the trap of lies is in learning, and improving through constant practice (just like learning to play golf or tennis), the ability to tell the truth.

We are all the walking wounded. Most of us are still interested in clarity and the truth, but at the same time we are interested in making a case for how our childhood was worse than average and how we're better than everyone else. The conventional way to suffer through life is to build a case for ourselves. That is what you get taught to value in Catholic parochial school and law school as well as all other schools (just not as efficiently as in those first two schools).

But at the same time we are all participants in a project to find out what being alive is. And when we lie or hide or avoid — essential tactics in case building — we don't discover anything new about life and we don't help others to discover anything new. Being interested in this common human project of discovery is an important part of the great conversation in which we humans have been engaged for several thousand years. For my own good, I want to hang out with people who want to find out what it would be like to live in such a way as to leave no unspoken words, no unfinished business; I want to be with people who are hungry for the truth, who want to spend time learning and sharing what they have learned rather than defending their images or reputations. This book is for that group of people that is growing larger every day — those whose thirst for knowledge and willingness to share overrides their defense against embarrassment. I am writing for people who want to grow beyond the adolescence that currently passes for adulthood, for the couples who are fed up with acting and blaming, for individuals interested in integrity or wholeness over moralism and fitting into roles. This book is an antidote to that conventional suffering. I hope it will piss you off and hurt you and inspire you, and break your mind's hold on your spirit. ॐ

I

The Being

MORALISM

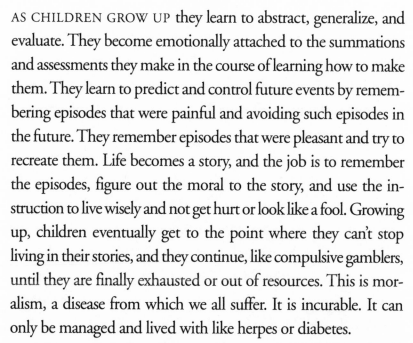

AS CHILDREN GROW UP they learn to abstract, generalize, and evaluate. They become emotionally attached to the summations and assessments they make in the course of learning how to make them. They learn to predict and control future events by remembering episodes that were painful and avoiding such episodes in the future. They remember episodes that were pleasant and try to recreate them. Life becomes a story, and the job is to remember the episodes, figure out the moral to the story, and use the instruction to live wisely and not get hurt or look like a fool. Growing up, children eventually get to the point where they can't stop living in their stories, and they continue, like compulsive gamblers, until they are finally exhausted or out of resources. This is moralism, a disease from which we all suffer. It is incurable. It can only be managed and lived with like herpes or diabetes.

Most people believe that morals are good and children should be given moral instruction. Most people raise their children to live in the jail of moralism in which they themselves live. Most teachers consider their main function to be teaching children to behave and do right and be conscientious. Every adult has a whole raft of values they think should be taught to children. Few of these people are conscious of the way in which the children are taught to value the values. Schools are central agents for transmission of the disease of moralism.

The disease of moralism in adults is characterized by hysterical faith in the mind. We are all sick to death from moralism. The world of human beings may die from it.

The passing on of learning from one generation to the next is not a bad design, and as an evolutionary development, it seems to have triumphed. The idea-generating, self-perpetuating machine that has evolved seems to have worked. Human beings have taken over the world. The ability to act based on accumulated information, and to pass great quantities of new information on, is the primary survival characteristic of the strongest animal on earth.

But, paradoxically, our survival mechanism has proved to be ultimately suicidal. It has allowed us to mass produce the consumables that provide us with the comfortable lifestyles that eventually kill us, to develop a technology for mass destruction of humans and the natural environment, and to rationalize the inexorable destruction of millions of lives relegated to fates of poverty, disease, and violence. Now we have to fix a few of our own glitches, perhaps in just a decade or two, or risk dying of our own evolution. Otherwise, human history may become just a little blip in time at the end of which technical design ability surpassed psycho-emotional evolution, eventually extinguishing the species.

Gregory Bateson says, in his calm, detached way, "Any species can get into an evolutionary cul-de-sac, and I suppose it is a mistake of sorts for that species to be a party to its own extinction. The human species, as we all know, may extinguish itself any day now."[1]

We have arrived at the evolutionary crisis of moralism. Our chances of living beyond this crisis of consciousness are, of course, unknown. Probably the odds are in favor of extermination of either the species, or the world that provides the context in which it lives, or both.

Managing the Disease of Moralism

Adult moralists are always angry people. The more the moralist is confronted with sloppy old experience, the more hysterical he or she becomes. We all get hysterical, but some of us lighten up and come to our senses more often than others. Some of us operate from hysterical moralism most of the time. Famous political moralists like Joseph McCarthy, Spiro Agnew, J. Edgar Hoover, and Hitler are great prototypes of the disease in our culture.

More lawyers come to me for therapy than do members of any other profession, and it's not coincidence, since so much of their training is to learn to live by rules. One important rule they try to live by is that the proper way to be angry is to have a fight using the rules. They often try to do this in their private lives, with complete lack of success. Perpetual arguing to convince others of the rightness of your case doesn't work worth a damn in personal relationships, and we all know it but can't seem to stop.

A law school education emphasizes the idiocy already built in by the culture. Law school begins with memorizing torts — formally learning the cases from the past and the principles they represent — and it gets worse as it goes on. After three years of law school a graduate usually takes the next step toward a law career: the bar exam for which he or she has to take a cram course to memorize cases, principles, generalizations, and values. When the exam is administered, the potential member of the bar knows in advance that he or she must score in the upper fifty percent of those taking the exam or fail. In the District of Columbia, if you are in the lower half of the group, but close to the cut-off, you may appeal your grade and request that your paper be regraded. However, they will not tell you the new grade until after the next bar exam has been administered. If you want to be sure you can go to work as a lawyer, you had better take the exam again even though you may have passed already. This is to teach you a lesson: do what you're told, no matter how ridiculous or unfair, if you want to be a lawyer. This continues, year after year, with the only apparent purpose being to make sure you have really learned to kiss ass in the culturally approved way.

Having passed the bar, if you are a high achiever, you then typically do a three- to seven-year stint of working 70 to 80 hours a week for a law firm trying to "make partner." After you have proven, through many additional trials, that you have learned to kiss ass in all circumstances, you may make partner. By the time you make partner you are a workaholic, so you keep up the pace out of habit, but also because you don't know what in the hell else to do in life but work and count principles.

This is the group from which we choose our political representatives. This is where judges come from. Though the learned disease of moralism is rampant in all professions, the middle-

aged lawyer is the quintessential prototype for this disease. Lawyers are the best representatives of the way people are today. They
are the mind of our culture.

One of the things that helps this disease of moral hysteria to
progress is detachment from identification of ourselves as our
experience. Hard physical work for the sake of survival used to
keep more people in touch with the world of being. As life becomes
less toil and more thinking and problem-solving, there is less
opportunity to have one's attention called forth from the mind
by more immediate demands of survival on a day-to-day basis.
The gap created by lack of grounding in our experience leaves us
dependent on ideas, principles, rules, values, and imagination as
our primary modes of orientation. These ideas and values are
tightly held in the same way an adolescent grasps onto roles when
he joins a gang or becomes a Christian or a Hare Krishna or falls
in love and gets married in high school. Without roles and rules
we fear we will lose control of ourselves. We will go crazy. We will
lose our minds. The more intensely these rules and roles are defended,
the further removed from grounding in experience the individual
becomes.

After enough practice at role-playing and idealism, our whole
way of orienting ourselves in the world depends on *principles of
orientation* rather than on the *ability to respond as needed* based on
what we perceive. This moralism, this web of entrapment of
human aliveness, is a crippling disease. We all have it. It is terminal. It cannot be cured. It's a hell of a lot worse than herpes. It is
as deadly as AIDS. It is in our schools. It is in our minds. It is in
the bloodstream of our culture. It is in this book.

Sometimes I receive letters from people who have heard that I am an expert in stress management. They ask me to suggest what they can do about stress and various psychosomatic disorders. They want recommendations about how to behave and what to do. I know when I write back that whatever I tell them probably won't work. Whatever advice I give them will be used as another principle to beat themselves over the head with, which is what caused the problem in the first place. Moralists who read about ways to beat stress only make those ways into new rules with which to oppress themselves. People who try to take a shit at 7:00 AM precisely every day whether they need to or not are different from people who take a shit when they feel like they need to. J. Edgar Hoover died of apoplexy. Maybe he popped a blood vessel in righteous indignation. I like to imagine he was reading a book on stress management at the time.

Field Independence versus Field Dependence
A number of experiments in the past thirty years have been designed to study what psychologists call "Field Dependence" and "Field Independence."[2]

Imagine this scene: A person is seated in a darkened room. Ten feet in front of this person (the subject) stands another person holding a luminescent square frame surrounding a luminescent straight rod. The room is darkened; all the subject can see is the frame and the rod. Both the frame and the rod are mounted on an axle, so they may each be rotated in both directions.

The person holding the frame and rod rotates both at random for a while. The frame is stopped and the rod continues

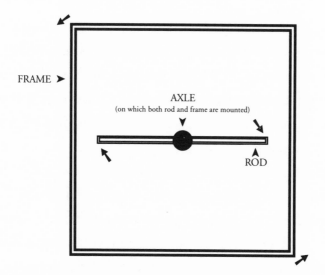

FRAME ➤

AXLE
(on which both rod and frame are mounted)

ROD

moving for a while. The person holding the rod and frame then says to the subject, "Tell me when the rod is straight up and down, the same as the walls outside."

Some people will make the rod straight up and down by using the square as a frame of reference. These people are called "field dependent" because they depend on the context or field provided by the frame to judge when the rod is perpendicular.

Other people line the rod straight up and down with regard to their own bodies. These people are called "field independent" because they operate independent of the square as a frame of reference.

Another variation of this experiment has the subject strapped into a tilting chair inside a room that tilts. Motors tilt both the room and chair and stop at some point at random. The subject is instructed to give verbal instructions to the operator of the motor that moves the chair to make himself line up straight. Field dependent subjects will tolerate up to a 33 degree angle of tilt and will say they are aligned with the walls outside *as long as they are tilted in the same direction as the room.* Like those who depend on the frame to judge the angle of the rod, these field dependent people depend on the tilt of the room to adjust the tilt of the chair in which they sit, even though their own bodies are telling them they are not sitting upright.

There is further research that demonstrates that field dependence is correlated with social dependence. Field dependent, socially dependent people take their cues from external frames of reference. Field independence is correlated with social independence and with creativity. Artists tend to be field independent. Those who learn to depend on rules rather than the seats of their pants, like Catholics and lawyers, tend to be field dependent. Catholic parochial school is an excellent method for the accomplishment of field dependence. Parochial school students, like law students, make better sheep than people. Catholic education and law schools provide me with a lot of miserable people as psychotherapy clients. I should be grateful. These people are looking for rescue from their education. The problem is they all want me to tell them what to do so they can try hard to do it, be better than anyone else at it, and get good grades so God will love them.

Depending on an external frame of reference for social orientation leads you to try to manipulate other people to get what you want rather than getting it on your own. What the well-trained field-dependent client usually does is try to con the therapist into telling him to do what he already wants to do — but is afraid of failing and getting blamed for — so if he fails, he can blame the authority who told him to do it.

Fritz Perls said in 1946, "Principles are substitutes for an independent outlook. The owner would be lost in the ocean of events if he were not able to orient himself by these fixed bearings. Usually he is even proud of them and does not regard them as weaknesses, but as a source of strength. He hangs on to them because of the insufficiency of his own independent judgment."[3]

We are all afraid to give up our moralism. We are afraid that if we do we will go out of control. We might do something bad, or bizarre, or crazy. We might go out of our minds.

Erik Erikson, in the biography, *Young Man Luther,* speculates that: "Some day, maybe, there will exist a well-informed, well considered, and yet fervent public conviction that the most deadly of all possible sins is the mutilation of a child's spirit; for such mutilation undercuts the life principle of trust, without which every human act, may it feel ever so good and seem ever so right, is prone to perversion by destructive forms of *conscientiousness* [emphasis mine]."[4] When we take innocent and open children and train them to be moralists, we train them at one and the same time to be liars. Moralism and lying go hand in hand. Being "good" and "looking good," conscientiously valued, lead directly to lying. If you can fool the nuns into believing you are good like they want you to be, you can secretly do what you want. Moral instruction, stringently imposed, tears children loose from their grounding in experience, from their trust of the world based on just being here, and makes them into conscientious, suffering torturers of the next generation. In Erikson's words, "The child, forced out of fear to pretend that he is better when seen than when unseen, is left to anticipate the day when he will have the brute power to make others more moral than he ever intends to be himself."[5]

The death-grip with which one holds on to principles is a source of unhappiness and anger. We can make a moral resolve that people *should* let up on themselves and other people, but that is just more impotent moralism.

If moralism is as common and influential in our society as I have described, how might one *use* the disease? That is, instead of attempting to cure it, how could we manage it and deal creatively with its use? *Managing* the disease of moralism is done by *telling the truth* like children do before they lose their innocence.

I have this disease. I want to use it rather than be used by it. How can I not just *manage* my critical, self-judgmental, mean-to-those-closest-to-me self, but use it to be happy, productive, and alive? My clients and friends and I have been having success in managing moralism by telling the truth.

The scary thing is that no one else can predict what will happen to *you* if you attempt to let up on your moralism. Only you can discover that, by abandoning the protection of your moralism in some way. Taking that risk is moving toward independence.

Self-reliance is field independence. Moral hysteria is field dependence. In the work I do, the most interesting questions are: can someone who has learned to be field dependent and socially dependent learn independence? Can moralism be transformed from a life-threatening disease to a managed one?

The answer to both questions is "Yes" — if the person is willing to tell the truth. ⤳

THE FIRST TRUTH

*"The world is my womb, and my
mother's womb was my first world."*
— R.D. Laing

WE GRADUALLY BEGIN to think of ourselves, in the course of growing up, as personalities made up of all the lessons we have learned. Our hard-earned lessons count heavily in our consideration of who we are. We complicate our lives by holding on to these hard-earned lessons long after they have outlived their usefulness. Take, for example, the child who learns to persistently beg his mother in a whiny voice, first for cookies, and later for the keys to the car. Since it worked with Mom, and since Dad left most of that up to Mom, he keeps using what works. At age 40, he may still be treating his third wife the same way without having gotten those same results for years. The mind doesn't like to change itself in the face of new information. Lessons learned and held on to in this fashion make up the personality to which we are shackled. This makes life harder than it has to be. The way out of this suffering is to expand who we consider ourselves to be. We must return to being more than the personalities we have shrunk to during the course of growing up.

By the time we are old enough to ride a bike we are personalities. In the course of learning to be personalities we forget something we knew before we had any vested interest in behaving consistently: that is, the common sense of unity in the womb, before we knew we existed.

These are my basic premises about how we all began: the earth happened by chance, and chemistry brought us to be. After a long period of evolution, you and I showed up. After about the first four or five months in the womb, we had our first experience of being: a dawning of consciousness.

The first experience we all had was when life came on. Dawn seems to be the best metaphor for this. Dawn happens in a slow and almost indistinguishable way, a long time before sunrise. The light of life came on for us, in the same way, a long time before birth. The Hindus call consciousness the light that enlightens the light, or the light that allows us to see light. In the womb is where this light, our consciousness, first occurred. For the first time we experienced *experience itself.* It happened like dawn, where the gradual accumulation of light makes it impossible to say when day has happened, but suddenly it is there. That is, we *were* our experience. The fetus matured until the wiring was complete and suddenly experiencing *was*. What we were in the womb was a unity of experiencing.

This unity of experience went on for an eternity. In our time, the time we know about now, it was four or five months. *Then* it was an eternity. Then it *was* eternity. We never forget that time, but we have no way of remembering it in a way we can describe.

It is indefinable, unrememberable in any graspable way. *All religions, gods, metaphysics, theologies, philosophies, and teachings of masters of all faiths are attempts to remember these eternal months past, this lost sense of unity.*

Since the beginning of human history, priests have been trying to put this sense of unity into words, trying to communicate about the ineffable. They knew something was there, but didn't know how to talk about it, yet couldn't resist trying. And the more they talked, the more confusion arose between the attempt to define unity and the actual experience of unity. As a result of our inability to put it into words, this experience of oneness, a commonplace experience, has become highly overrated.

Enlightenment is *knowing* unity, not being able to talk about it. The *philosophy* of enlightenment is talking about or trying to describe the experience of unity.

Unity is the nature of things. It doesn't take any work. It is the given. We are each creators of the universe out of our own being. What is given us to experience is a unity, within which we make distinctions. The sound we hear when our ears are stopped up is the electrical generator of unity. When our eyes are closed the darkness we see is the generator of unity. When our eyes are open whatever we see is who we actually are. As Krishnamurti says, "you are the world."[1] From the moment life starts, the *being* we are constantly creates the world with its senses. The world grows and the mind grows out of this unity. The world is created for us out of our fundamental equipment — our being.

We are constantly creating the world by merely perceiving. When we hear, we are creating sound. When we see, we are creating what is seen in our visual cortex. When we integrate sight, sound, smell, touch, balance, movement, etc., our involuntary nervous system creates the world. When we die, for all practical purposes, the world ends. We are, nevertheless, each creators of the world. But since we do it effortlessly, and everybody does it, it doesn't count for much in our considerations of who we are. Usually we consider creating *meaning* to be more important than creating the world. We take for granted our function as creators of the world and focus much more attention on creating meaning. We are preoccupied with the power of interpretation. We are much more interested in our uniqueness, derived from what we have worked to learn, than in the source of our power as creators.

It is our fate as human beings to grasp after the ineffable, trying to regain a lost sense of unity. Even so, when we do get in touch with unity, the vastness of our being, for a few seconds, we usually run. We feel as if we are about to lose something. We are. We are about to lose the protection and safety of the limited definition of self we have come to *think* we are. We are afraid of losing who we think we are, which is special, and we are afraid of becoming who we actually are, which is *not* special.

When we become aware of ourselves as indefinable, uncategorizeable, simple, creators of the world, we lose all certainty. Being present to the immediate moment-to-moment passing of the world, the fragility of our own being, and the relative unimportance of the personality we think we are, is a terrifying experience. Being fully aware of our ever-present, ever-changing existence throws us into the same ineffable state as when the light came on while we were unseeing in the womb. Simultaneous awareness of the life of being, and the lesser importance of the personality to which we have become attached, is a second enlightenment, that comes to all humans who grow up beyond the stage of adolescence. But it feels like dying. To avoid the trauma of it, the great majority of us remain adolescents until the end of our lives.

This is not a minor philosophical point. This is the heart of the matter. Most of us would rather kill ourselves than *be*, particularly if who we think we are keeps dying. Many of us do.

The Birth of Being

Go back for a moment in your imagination and memory to the beginning: there are sounds like intestines rumbling, sensations are stirring, and there is a vague sense of movement and other sounds, like dolphins calling to each other under the sea. In this beginning, there is no seeing, thus no dark. To the unborn there is no knowledge of darkness because there is no light and no mind to contrast dark and light. Experiences in this unseeing world begin to form the mind.

Here, in a "background" which is all that we are, which lasts however long we do, we *are* our beginning. You can go back here anytime you like. I often do when I meditate.

Much later, a true eternity later, the experiences of birth, light, air, breathing and pain flood the being.

The mind is born out of this ocean of experience — before and after birth. Even after seven months in the womb, the unborn baby is capable of learning to respond in a predictable fashion to outside stimuli, such as sound. Laboratory experiments have found that a seven-month-old fetus will react to an electrical shock to the mother's womb with a full contraction. When this shock is applied along with a loud sound, the fetus is conditioned, after only a few trials, to go into a full contraction at the loud sound, without any electrical shock. An association between the sound and shock is made; therefore learning has occurred. So now we know (thanks to evil scientists who have tortured fetuses in this manner), that the mind begins to form, from associations between ebbs and flows in the ocean of experience, prior to birth. This grouping of replicated experiences begins to form the mind.

Sometime shortly after birth we demarcate a little area, a smaller sea, from our ocean of experience. Our mother's breast, our mother, our hand, our body, our clothes, our bed, our room get distinguished for us. We become a sea of suggestions. We grow up all the rest of the way surrounded and protected by this expanding sea of suggestions, and eventually, thousands of refinements later, a group of suggestions becomes who we *think* we are.

Who we *actually* are, of course, remains always more than the mental images we form while growing up. First we are the experiencer of what is momentarily present; second we are the multi-sensory recorder of experience; last, and less importantly, we are the rememberer. Later, we are most focused on remembering our own reputations. But who we always really are, from the beginning, is a context, a parenthesis, a being who creates the world for itself by sensing. We are the Being who is the source of being and remembering. Re-contacting that basic beginning electrical sensate self rescues us from the mind — the murderer, and potential ally, within.

Getting Born Again

As you may recall, we have a lot to deal with in order to grow up all the way to adulthood. After forming a personality and losing touch with the wholeness of being, we then rediscover wholeness, but experience it as a threat to our personality. Personality can eventually be included in the wholeness of being, but not without some hard work that requires courage and takes a while. It is a process of disintegration and reintegration. Some people call it dying and getting born again.

The creator being is the being that came alive in the womb at about four or five months after conception when the wiring was complete and the light came on. We forget this being rather quickly. In just a few years we are so surrounded by our creation, the sea of suggestions, we can hardly touch or taste or smell or feel or see the ocean of experience that still surrounds us. We forget we live in a sea that is a part of an ocean at all. We forget we are the source of the whole ocean. Getting born again is remembering that.

To summarize: we awaken in the womb into an ocean of experience. Over a long period of time, that ocean of experience becomes a sea of suggestions. We lose track of the ocean of experience. We lose track of having created the sea.

After we have lost track of everything sufficiently, we continue to interact with the sea and create a self. What we call the "self" is a creation of further interactions of the sea of suggestions. The being we were when we began, the being we actually still are, alive in an ocean of experience, including all the ocean as itself, recedes to the background of our attention, and the "self" we have created comes to the foreground. As we identify with our newly created self, we lose touch with the being we are and have been since the light came on.

All religious experiences can be accounted for by a kind of yearning to recapture completely the four-to-nine month time-lapse photograph of being we developed in that eternal time in the womb. A kind of fused multi-sensory recording, made before our senses themselves were distinct, before birth, resides in each of our memories; a remembrance of unity. This undistinguished unity lasts some time past birth until the baby breaks the world into two pieces with its first conception based on replicated events. That first conception may have come after being fed at mother's breast many times. At some point the memory of previous events of warmth, milk, cuddling, sucking, swallowing becomes distinguished from all other memories, and the baby cries to be fed. At that point, if the baby gets fed and remembers it, the next time the baby is hungry and cries again, he or she enters time and a life of increasing distinctions. The global world of experience becomes divided into "feeding events" and "non-feeding events." The unity we all search for, the peace that passeth understanding and the looked-forward-to heaven and reunion with God, is a vague but all-pervasive memory of a time of bliss, yearningly remembered from the past, and longingly projected forward to the future.

This yearning for something that can't quite be remembered in the way we usually remember is constantly triggered by the ever-present background experience of being. When we close our eyes and cover our ears, we can hear our own heartbeat and hum. It stimulates remembrances of times past that can't be conceptualized. From thee we come. To thee we go.

There is a Zen story about two fishes arguing about the existence of the ocean. The first fish says, "It's all around you. You are surrounded by it. You are surrounded by water. You have lived in water all of your life." "Show me! Prove it! Where is this ocean?" the second fish demands. This difficulty in being aware of the perpetual, continuous, taken-for-granted, sustenance of being is that it has been there since the light first came on. We have nothing with which to compare it; no measure of its existence.

The ever-present ocean of experience has no inside or outside. Inside us and outside us are both inside us. Who we are is the Being within which occurs that experience we call "inside our body" and that experience we call "outside our body." More accurately, we are the inside and outside experience itself, happening. We learn "inside" and "outside" an eternity after the light first comes on (because then we had no concept of time) and years after we are born. (It takes an eternity plus a couple of years before our minds distinguish "inside" and "outside.")

The mind is the sea of suggestions we learned as we grew. The mind is born out of the indefinable ocean of experience we first were and still are. The sea of suggestions we come to *think* we are as personalities is itself in a larger ocean, like the original ocean of experience, currently obscured by the sea of suggestions we consider ourselves to be.

To be *whole,* we must recontact the being we are and were and evermore shall be until the end of each of our times. That being is the creator being — the background hum that keeps us cooking, the basic circuit board, the baseline buzz. The cognitive faculties of the mind are a secondary development for steering, not the primary driving force of life. Minds are developed and lead us away from the experience of being, and religious practices were developed to get us back to it. All religions were developed to help us get back home to the hum we started with.

Meditation, sitting quietly until the mind settles down, brings a sense of wholeness. I believe the primary value of meditation is that, while meditating, we reunify the memory of our first sense of being with our current breathing, heart-beating, sensate, present-tense experience of being. Being a living being, "knowing" in our bones that we have been being for some time, is the heart of who each of us is. *We are beings alive behind the mask of personality.* Sitting in the Zendo (a place of meditation), that is what we find when we let ourselves be.

Marilyn Ferguson, for years the editor of *Brain/Mind* magazine and author of *The Aquarian Conspiracy,* says, "Those who want direct knowledge, the mystics, have always been treated more or less as heretics.... Now the heretics are gaining ground, doctrine is losing its authority, and knowledge is superseding belief."[2] Mystics are people who rediscover experience. Belief is the sea of suggestions about who we think we are. The path from doctrine to knowledge is a development beyond doctrine. Psychotherapy was invented to try to keep body and soul together — to help us to not mind being all the time and to not be minding all the time.

In the course of growing to adult size, we all have to learn the roles and rules. In order to do this, we forget, subsume, take for granted, ignore, or drop consciousness of our essential being. The path to the good life leads on further than childhood moralism, but a lot of people don't go that far. The path from doctrine to heresy is a natural growth — a natural evolution — a transition from one level of maturity to another. Very few of us stay on the path, however, because we get so damaged by those who teach us the doctrine. We become so filled with hate, and so embroiled in arguments and entangled in the webs of our minds that we stop growing. With rare exceptions, up until and including the present time in history, this has been the case for all human beings.

We can no longer afford the luxury of waiting for what might naturally evolve over time: a way to not damage all the children so badly. We are in danger of damaging ourselves to death. The problem, formerly serious, has become critical. The sentimental, idealistic romanticism of deeply felt religious belief, though responsible for the suffering of millions, was relatively harmless until we developed hydrogen bombs and other world-threatening technology. We can no longer afford to sit around in groups together to indulge in a tearful remembering forward, of a forgotten hoped-for sense of unity, at the direction of various priests and patrolmen who would have us gear up to attack other groups doing the same thing. We must grow beyond where human beings were for all of those years of recalling and hoping for paradise. Because of the various doomsday scenarios for the fate of the earth, we must make a sudden advance in consciousness or perish. Unless more human beings expand who they consider themselves to be, by re-including what they excluded when they grew a personality — unless more of us grow beyond the ignorant provincialism of adolescent moralizing — the game is over. Like rats behind the Pied Piper, we will follow our leaders off the cliff and back into the sea forever. ⋍

II

The Mind

3

THE BEING BECOMES DOMINATED
BY THE MIND

*"Children guessed (but only a few)
and down they forgot as up they grew..."*
— e.e. cummings

CHILDREN LOSE THEIR INNOCENCE from being repeatedly hurt in the natural course of life, even if they do not have abusive parents. If the adults who surround a child are intent on *teaching* them, the open innocence of childhood is even more quickly obliterated. Hatred is passed on from generation to generation through what we teach children "for their own good." The survival and progress of mankind has occurred through the learning of little children. The brainwashing that human acculturation is, concerning who we are and how we should behave, gets transmitted to the new member in a culture as he or she grows from birth to adolescence. Most of this occurs unthinkingly. We just somehow know how to raise our kids and what we should teach them based on our memories of how we were raised. Our resolves to be like or not like our parents, or to have our kids turn out like us or not like us, have very little to do with the full cultural programming.

It is in the nature of human beings to learn to abstract and generalize more and more as they grow older. In any group of people, minds grow that way. The group encourages and supports certain perspectives, and that is what a culture is. The more forcefully certain points of view are inculcated by any given set of parents and other teachers, the more hatred is built into the character structure of the acculturated individual, who then passes the taboos and resentment on to the next generation.

Parents, out of a confused mixture of fear, love and anger, try to care for children the best they can, using the mind-sets they have been given by their own parents. They constantly warn their children to be careful, do this, don't do that, and watch out for a dangerous world. The results for millions of us have been tragic. We have been taught to be paranoid and guarded in life as our parents' way of trying to ensure our survival after they are gone. In turn, we attempt to convince our own children of the correctness of believing in the rules of safety, so that they will act according to the principles we teach them. We teach them how to be good according to our morals, then to believe in moralism, then to moralize. It's important to us to stringently dictate protective rules and to instill faith in the necessity of rules for control of self and others.

In our present culture, we are changing our minds a little bit about the use of rules. The change is very difficult for us. I have been witnessing the beginnings of this change and later on in this book I will tell you some stories that reflect this change. This book is itself the result of our culture slowly changing its collective mind.

How tenaciously children and adolescents cling to the values, beliefs, abstractions, and generalizations that they learn depends on how disturbed they are at the time the learning occurs. The amount of displaced anger, grief, sexuality, or joy being suppressed at that time has a big effect on both *what* they learn and *how* they learn. In any given culture, the brainwashed ones who fit in best (lawyers and teachers) assume much of the leadership. As a culture burns out or fails to renew itself through change, its educational and political leaders are often the least creative members — the ones who cling hysterically to old methods simply because they once worked. The best people in a dying culture are the outcasts considered crazy by the leaders; the ones most disillusioned with their own culture. In Yeats' phrase, "the best lack all conviction, while the worst are full of passionate intensity."[1] Intense emotional attachment to any value, any virtue, any set of "shoulds" is a disease, a mental illness, a condition of self-murder and cultural assassination. I call this disease *moralism.*

Planting the Seeds of Moralism

A picture on the front page of the *Chicago Sun-Times* shows a uniformed policewoman carrying a young child out through an apartment door. The child, who is about four years old, is bruised and bleeding with one eye swollen shut. She is reaching back over the policewoman's shoulder and crying hysterically, trying to go back to her mother who has just beaten her so badly. The story reports that the mother claims to have beaten her little girl because she was bad, and that the little girl was screaming when she left, "Please don't take me away. I'll be good! I'll be good!"

The poor little thing probably thought that being taken away from her mother was further punishment for some way in which she was deeply bad and wrong.

Children try very hard to do what their parents want. Most of us suffered a lot in childhood from believing that something must be wrong with us, or our parents wouldn't be so unhappy. The story of this child's abuse in the *Sun-Times* is a graphic picture of the kind of trap childhood is for most children, even those who are not physically abused — even those whose parents believe they are being kind. The suffering of children abused by moralism, which is so common as to hardly be noticed, is based on the same desperate trying and wanting to please parents — to survive and be good enough to keep, and be worthy of their love — displayed by the little girl in the photograph.

Moralism is a disease in which "good" and "bad" become more important than "alive" or "dead." The heart of the disease is hurt and anger and fear of losing love and hysterical hope that we can somehow figure out how to be good enough to keep hurts from happening again.

In this quest, *control* is one of the first things children learn that they need to learn. That was just one of those things we found out when we grew up: we needed to get control of ourselves. But the imposition of control is often the source of anger. The imposition of control on anger is the source of even greater anger. Displacement of anger in the form of judgments and internal moral resolves results in the child learning to hate everybody else and eventually himself as well. The growing child learns this as a way to survive.

Katherine Anne Porter's short story *The Downward Path to Wisdom*,[2] from which excerpts follow, is a fine example of the way family traditions of hatred are stored and transferred and how hatred is passed on as "concern" or even "love." *The Downward Path to Wisdom* is the story of a child learning to survive and protect himself for the rest of his life. It depicts how the little sea of cultural suggestions in the teensy head of a little oppressed being gets made into a life-long personality.

In the story, four-year-old Stephen went to stay with his Grandma after having been abruptly taken from his parents during an argument involving him. He was rushed from the scene of conflict by Marjory, his parent's maid, and deposited at Grandma's. A few days later, he started school. He met little Frances at school and won her friendship by providing her with balloons that he had innocently filched from his Uncle David. In this scene, Frances and Stephen play one Saturday morning while her nurse visits with Stephen's caretaker, Old Janet.

> The nurse and Old Janet sat in Old Janet's room drinking coffee and gossiping, and the children sat on the side porch blowing balloons. Stephen chose an apple-colored one and Frances a pale green one. Between them on the bench lay a tumbled heap of delights still to come.
>
> "I once had a silver balloon," said Frances, "a beyootiful silver one, not round like these; it was a long one. But these are even nicer, I think," she added quickly, for she did want to be polite.

"When you get through with that one," said Stephen, gazing at her with the pure bliss of giving added to loving, "you can blow up a blue one and then a pink one and a yellow one and a purple one." He pushed the heap of limp objects toward her. Her clear-looking eyes, with fine little rays of brown in them like the spokes of a wheel, were full of approval for Stephen. "I wouldn't want to be greedy, though, and blow up all your balloons."

"There'll be plenty more left," said Stephen, and his heart rose under his thin ribs. He felt his ribs with his fingers and discovered with some surprise that they stopped somewhere in front, while Frances sat blowing balloons rather halfheartedly. The truth was, she was tired of balloons. After you blow six or seven your chest gets hollow and your lips feel puckery. She had been blowing balloons steadily for three days now. She had begun to hope they were giving out. "There's boxes and boxes more of them, Frances," said Stephen happily. "Millions more. I guess they'd last and last if we didn't blow too many every day."

Frances said somewhat timidly, "I tell you what. Let's rest awhile and fix some liquish water. Do you like liquish?"

"Yes, I do," said Stephen, "but I haven't got any."

"Couldn't we buy some?" asked Frances. "It's only a cent a stick, the nice rubbery, twisty kind. We can put it in a bottle with some water, and shake it and shake it, and it makes foam on top like soda pop and we can drink it. I'm kind of thirsty," she said in a small, weak voice. "Blowing balloons all the time makes you thirsty, I think."

Stephen, in silence, realized a dreadful truth and a numb feeling crept over him. He did not have a cent to buy a licorice for Frances and she was tired of his balloons. This was the first real dismay of his whole life, and he aged at least a year in the next minute, huddled, with his deep, serious blue eyes focused down his nose in intense speculation. What could he do to please Frances that would not cost money? Only yesterday Uncle David had given him a nickel, and he had thrown it away on gumdrops. He regretted that nickel so bitterly his neck and forehead were damp. He was thirsty too.

"I tell you what," he said, brightening with a splendid idea, lamely trailing off on second thought, "I know something we can do, I'll–I..."

"I am thirsty," said Frances with gentle persistence. "I think I'm so thirsty maybe I'll have to go home." She did not leave the bench, though, but sat, turning her grieved mouth toward Stephen.

Stephen quivered with the terrors of the adventure before him, but he said boldly, "I'll make some lemonade. I'll get sugar and lemon and some ice and we'll have lemonade."

"Oh, I love lemonade," cried Frances. "I'd rather have lemonade than liquish."

"You stay right here," said Stephen, "and I'll get

everything."

He ran around the house, and under Old Janet's window he heard the dry, chattering voices of the two old women whom he must outwit. He sneaked on tiptoe to the pantry, took a lemon lying there by itself, a handful of lump sugar and a china teapot, smooth, round, with flowers and leaves all over it. These he left on the kitchen table while he broke a piece of ice with a sharp metal pick he had been forbidden to touch. He put the ice in the pot, cut the lemon and squeezed it as well as he could — a lemon was tougher and more slippery than he had thought — and mixed sugar and water. He decided there was not enough sugar so he sneaked back and took another handful. He was back on the porch in an astonishingly short time, his face tight, his knees trembling, carrying a pitcher with iced lemonade in it, and his grandma or Old Janet might walk through the door at any moment.

"Come on, Frances," he whispered loudly. "Let's go round to the back behind the rose bushes where it's shady." Frances leaped up and ran like a deer beside him, her face wise with knowledge of why they ran; Stephen ran stiffly, cherishing his teapot with clenched hands.

It was shady behind the rose bushes, and much safer. They sat side by side on the dampish ground, legs doubled under, drinking in turn from the slender spout. Stephen took his just share in large, cool, delicious swallows. When Frances drank she set her round pink mouth daintily to the spout and her throat beat steadily as a heart. Stephen was thinking he had really done something pretty nice for Frances. He did not know where his own happiness was; it was mixed with the sweet-sour taste in his mouth and a cool feeling in his bosom because Frances was there drinking his lemonade which he had got for her with great danger.

Frances said, "My, what big swallows you take," when his turn came next.

"No bigger than yours," he told her downrightly. "You take awfully big swallows."

"Well," said Frances, turning this criticism into an argument for her rightness about things, "that's the way to drink lemonade anyway." She peered into the teapot. There was quite a lot of lemonade left and she was beginning to feel she had enough. "Let's make up a game and see who can take the biggest swallows."

This was such a wonderful notion they grew reckless, tipping the spout into their opened mouths above their heads until lemonade welled up and ran over their chins in rills down their fronts. When they tired of this there was still lemonade left in the pot. They played first at giving the rosebush a drink and ended by baptizing it. "Name father son holygoat," shouted Stephen, pouring. At this sound Old Janet's face appeared over the low hedge, with the tan, disgusted-looking face of Frances' nurse hanging over her shoulder.

"Well, just as I thought," said Old Janet. "Just as I expected." The bag under her chin waggled.

"We were thirsty," he said; "we were awfully thirsty." Frances said nothing, but she gazed steadily at the toes of her shoes.

"Give me that teapot," said Old Janet, taking it with a rude snatch. "Just because you're thirsty is no reason," said Old Janet. "You can ask for things. You don't have to steal."

"We didn't steal," cried Frances suddenly. "We didn't. We didn't!"

"That's enough from you, missy," said her nurse. "Come straight out of there. You have nothing to do with this."

"Oh, I don't know," said Old Janet with a hard stare at Frances' nurse. "He never did such a thing before, by himself."

"Come on," said the nurse to Frances, "this is no place for you." She held Frances by the wrist and started walking away so fast Frances had to run to keep up. "Nobody can call us thieves and get away with it."

"You don't have to steal, even if others do," said Old Janet to Stephen, in a high carrying voice. "If you so much as pick up a lemon in somebody else's house you're a little thief." She lowered her voice and said "Now I'm going to tell your grandma and you'll see what you get."

"He went in the icebox and left it open," Janet told

Grandma, "and he got into the lump sugar and spilt it all over the floor. Lumps everywhere underfoot. He dribbled water all over the clean kitchen floor, and he baptized the rose bush, blaspheming. And he took your Spode teapot."

"I didn't either," said Stephen loudly, trying to free his hand from Old Janet's big hard fist.

"Don't tell fibs," said Old Janet; "that's the last straw."

"Oh, dear," said Grandma. "He's not a baby any more." She shut the book she was reading and pulled the wet front of his pullover toward her. "What's this sticky stuff on him?" she asked and straightened her glasses.

"Lemonade," said Old Janet. "He took the last lemon."

They were in the big dark room with the red curtains. Uncle David walked in from the room with the bookcases, holding a box in his uplifted hand. "Look here," he said to Stephen. "What's become of all my balloons?"

Stephen knew well that Uncle David was not really asking a question.

Stephen, sitting on a footstool at his grandma's knee, felt sleepy. He leaned heavily and wished he could put his head on her lap, but he might go to sleep, and it would be wrong to go to sleep while Uncle David was still talking. Uncle David walked about the room with his hands in his pockets, talking to Grandma. Now and then he would walk over to a lamp and, leaning, peer into the top of the shade, winking in the light, as if he expected to find something there.

"It's simply in the blood, I told her," said Uncle David. "I told her she would simply have to come and get him, and keep him. She asked me if I meant to call him a thief and I said if she could think of a more exact word I'd be glad to hear it."

"You shouldn't have said that," commented Grandma calmly.

"Why not? She might as well know the facts...I suppose he can't help it," said Uncle David, stopping now in front of Stephen and dropping his chin into his collar, "I shouldn't expect too much of him, but you can't begin too early—"

"The trouble is," said Grandma, and while she spoke she took Stephen by the chin and held it up so that he had to meet her eye; she talked steadily in a mournful tone, but Stephen could not understand. She ended, "It's not just about the balloons, of course."

"It is about the balloons," said Uncle David angrily, "because balloons now mean something worse later. But what can you expect? His father — well, it's in the blood. He–"

"That's your sister's husband you're talking about," said Grandma, "and there is no use making things worse. Besides, you don't really know."

"I do know," said Uncle David. And he talked again

very fast, walking up and down. Stephen tried to understand, but the sounds were strange and floating just over his head. They were talking about his father, and they did not like him. Uncle David came over and stood above Stephen and Grandma. He hunched over them with a frowning face, a long, crooked shadow from him falling across them to the wall. To Stephen he looked like his father, and he shrank against his grandma's skirts.

"The question is, what to do with him now?" asked Uncle David. "If we keep him here, he'd just be a — I won't be bothered with him. Too far gone already, I'm afraid. No training. No example."

"You're right, they must take him and keep him," said Grandma. She ran her hands over Stephen's head; tenderly she pinched the nape of his neck between thumb and forefinger. "You're your Grandma's darling," she told him, "and you've had a nice long visit, and now you're going home. Mama is coming for you in a few minutes. Won't that be nice?"

"I want my mama," said Stephen, whimpering, for his grandma's face frightened him. There was something wrong with her smile.

Oppressed and distressed by his caretakers' angry, principled attempts to improve his flawed moral character, the little boy struggles to defend himself against the emotional onslaught in which he knows he is unsafe. His mother arrives, argues bitterly with her brother David, and attempts through false cheer and bravado to protect her son. As the story ends, Stephen demonstrates the perversely logical strategy employed by oppressed human beings throughout history to protect themselves against torturers of all sorts: imitation.

"Come on, Stephen darling," said Mama. "It's far past his bedtime," she said, to no one in particular. "Imagine keeping a baby up to torture him about a few miserable little bits of colored rubber." She smiled at Uncle David with both rows of teeth as she passed him on the way to the door, keeping between him and Stephen. "Ah, where would we be without high moral standards," she said, and then to Grandma, "Good night, Mother," in quite her usual voice. "I'll see you in a day or so."

"Yes, indeed," said Grandma cheerfully, coming out into the hall with Stephen and Mama. "Let me hear from you. Ring me up tomorrow. I hope you'll be feeling better."

"I feel very well now," said Mama brightly, laughing. She bent down and kissed Stephen. "Sleepy, darling? Papa's waiting to see you. Don't go to sleep until you've kissed your papa good night."

Stephen woke with a sharp jerk. He raised his head and put out his chin a little. "I don't want to go home," he said; "I want to go to school. I don't want to see Papa, I don't like him."

Mama laid her palm over his mouth softly. "Darling, don't."

Uncle David put his head out with a kind of snort. "There you are, he said. "There you've got a statement from headquarters."

Mama opened the door and ran, almost carrying Stephen. She ran across the sidewalk, jerking open the car door and dragging Stephen in after her. She spun the car around and dashed forward so sharply Stephen was almost flung out of the seat. He sat braced then with all his might, hands digging into the cushions. The car speeded up and the trees and houses whizzed by all flattened out. Stephen began suddenly to sing to himself, a quiet, inside song so Mama would not hear. He sang his new secret; it was a comfortable, sleepy song: "I hate Papa, I hate Mama, I hate Grandma, I hate Uncle David, I hate Old Janet, I hate Marjory, I hate Papa I hate Mama..."

His head bobbed, leaned, came to rest on Mama's knee, eyes closed. Mama drew him closer and slowed down, driving with one hand.

Oppression masked as "concern" provokes in the child a response of hatred, severing of communication, and withdrawal of relationship with those closest to him. This a typical stage in a child's training for survival in the adult world, and a step towards the diminishment of aliveness. After being loved, and being surprised with hurt and being blamed, Stephen learned to blame. Stephen blamed his uncle, his grandmother, Old Janet, and Marjory for tormenting him for his mistakes, which were natural, venturesome initiatives on his part; and for his apparent resemblance to his parents whom he also hates for being the original causes of disgust for him in the other adults. He is learning to have good causes for hatred, just like they do. He is learning to be like them in order to survive among them. *The Downward Path to Wisdom* is about all of us. When little Stephen started singing his hate song it was a metaphor for the hate songs we all learn. Our liberation from the hatred and isolation of the mental jail that we, like Stephen, began constructing in childhood, depends on our willingness to knock down the walls and resume relationship to others. When we do this we invite the reawakening of all the pain and shock of the original wounds inflicted on us in our innocence, against which we defended ourselves with the resolve to hate. Telling the truth, after hiding out for a long time, reopens old wounds that didn't heal properly. It often hurts a lot. It takes guts. It isn't easy. It is better than the alternative. ⌒

4

LEVELS OF TELLING THE TRUTH

"Oh, but I was so much older then;
I'm younger than that now."
— Bob Dylan

KATHLEEN WAS 35 YEARS OLD and head of her own business; hard working, competent, pretty, and bright — a survivor. Her business was going great and she was getting rich. She came to me because, in spite of the appearance of great success, she was hypertensive, unable to have orgasms, suffering from insomnia and asthma, frenetic about work, and depressed about not having any intimate relationships with men. She came from a large Catholic family. She had been stuck in early adolescence for years and was destined to stay there for the remainder of her life, as many parochial school students do, having learned from the nuns that the most important thing in life was to put on an act for parents and overseers and live your real life on the side. You have a public life and a secret life; keep it that way.

Eight years earlier, she had gotten an abortion — ironically, on a weekend when her parents were marching in a right-to-life demonstration. She had told no one about it except the man who impregnated her, and she had soon broken up with him. She had guarded her secret well through two years of individual psychotherapy with another therapist and many intensive groups where there had been opportunities for telling the truth. First she told me. Then she told members of a therapy group. Then she told her friends. Then she told her sister. Each increment of revelation brought a degree of self-forgiveness and freedom. Each increment of lightening up about her dark secret helped quite a bit, but it wasn't enough. I encouraged her to finish with the matter by telling the truth to her parents. She resisted for some time, and finally I told her she had either to do it or get out of therapy. She agreed to tell them.

She made several trips home with the intention of having a completely honest conversation with her folks, but she would get scared and come back without having spoken a word. After many failed attempts, she finally told her parents about the abortion. Because of the number of times she had gone home and retreated without telling, the first thing her father said when she finally came out with it was "Oh, thank God," because he and her mother had already secretly concluded that Kathleen probably had a terminal disease she couldn't bring herself to tell them about. After the topic was broached and a discussion ensued about why Kathleen and all the other children lied to them all of the time, the brother who was in town was called over, and the family had quite a long discussion about who everyone was, about lying and about the games the kids had played with the parents and the secrets they had kept among themselves. This conversation with her family was a breakthrough in her psychotherapy.

Kathleen no longer has asthma. A few months after that trip home, she began living with a man to whom she is now married. She has orgasms almost every time they have sex. She can sleep. She runs her business and takes time off as she likes. She is even more successful but not miserable anymore. She has accomplished the first level of telling the truth.

Kathleen stepped out from behind her "good daughter" role, which she had maintained by hiding and lying all of the time, risked her relationship to her parents for the sake of revealing who she really was, and ended up transforming not only her own way of being in the world but that of her whole family.

Roles are like clothing we learned to put on to protect ourselves from the cold. When we take off the roles we have been hiding behind, the naked being we are stands there — vulnerable and defenseless. The *being* we are, as distinct from the *roles* we've been playing, doesn't need the defensive weapons we invented to scare the enemy away. Those other people out there are naked under their roles too — they are playing possum, or creating a stink, or baring their fangs and growling, or signaling anger and threatening like a chimp, or running like a rabbit. Their roles were developed for the sake of survival, just as our roles were.

The difference between our survival tactics and those of animals is that theirs are necessary for the continuation of their physical existence, and ours are not. But we act as though ours were. We conceal ourselves because we fear that the pain accompanying the act of self-disclosure will literally destroy us, or fundamentally damage our being in some horrible way, rendering us maimed and dysfunctional. In addition, we fear we may destroy *others* with our truth-telling. Kathleen recoiled for years from what she saw as the utterly destructive power of her unleashed secret — it would, she thought, "kill" her parents and herself to have it told. But telling the truth kills nothing but false roles, images, interpretations, and lies, as Kathleen discovered. It only kills those deceits which we had kept alive through strategic self-concealment. "Kathleen," — her false image — did *not* survive her revelation. But Kathleen did. Through telling the truth, she revealed herself, and thus delivered herself and her family into a new and more powerful relationship, achieved through the death of the old, lying relationship.

The ability to "get naked" in front of other people who are still in their roles, as Kathleen did, is important. Coming out from behind our roles permits us to look behind the roles of others. Because we can see more clearly, the threat of other people, posing in their roles, fades. Once we come out from behind our pose, what used to scare us about other people doesn't scare us anymore. Coming off it, dropping the roles we thought we needed for protection, turns out to be not only safe, but a place of power. Kathleen got less scared of other people, particularly men.

Intimacy is a power grown into after adolescence. The person capable of intimacy — that is, the person capable of telling the truth — still has roles to play, but is no longer trapped by them. The integrated person behind the role no longer has anything to hide, and can relate freely to the being he knows is hidden behind the roles others are playing. The *person* is then in charge, rather than the role.

I differentiate three phases, or levels, of telling the truth. These levels may occur successively, or simultaneously, or a person may master one or two levels and retreat from the next. Often people retreat after encountering the frightening sense of freedom afforded by a breakthrough at a new level. Sometimes they try again later, sometimes not. The three levels are: revealing the facts; honestly expressing current feelings and thoughts; and, finally, exposing the fiction you have devised to represent yourself and your history.

Level One: Revealing the Facts

Kathleen is an example of level one of telling the truth. The first level of telling the truth is to reveal the facts. It is a matter of clearing up lies from the past and the false presentation of self being maintained through withholding.

We all lie casually and habitually and are largely unconscious about it. We all learned to lie innocently, as we learned the ways of being "grown up" and how to impress our friends. We have to develop and organize the lies we pretend to be, and complete that job, and feel O.K. about it, before we can give up that identity. We have to strut and pose and try on lots of roles and tell a lot of lies and do a good job of it before giving it up. But if we continue to grow, we *will* give the roles up. Eventually we can joke about what used to be serious work in learning how to represent ourselves to others. That ability to joke about who we are comes only after we have developed the basic identity (the fundamental lie) we think we are. Then, despite all that work, we have to give up our attachment to that identity. If we don't, we'll never be free from its restrictions.

Here is another way of saying it. We have to go through adolescence and develop an identity, and answer the question, "Who am I?" Having established that identity, we have to give up our attachment to it, and remember who we were, at the beginning, before we developed that identity. Who we still are (the being from back in the womb), and who we have come to know ourselves as (the identity we have developed), have to be integrated. Then, when we relate to other people, we can come from a consciousness of our whole being and the being of others and *have* a personality, rather than *be had* by our personality.

The first level of this process is revealing deceptions and withholds. You have been maintaining an image in the eyes of others to sell yourself to them in a certain way. Now you have to untell those lies. If you never have told your mother and father that you stole the car at 1:00 AM to visit your boyfriend when you were 16, go tell them and face the consequences even if you are 40. It must be done.

Linda's case illustrates a retreat from this first level of telling the truth:

Linda is a 37-year-old woman raised in the Midwest in a middle-class, Protestant home. All of her life, the point of living has been to be good and not bad, to score points, to be a star in high school and college, to make As, and to be well thought of. She was a cheerleader and a member of all the important clubs in high school and college. She is very successful and makes a lot of money and is highly regarded in her profession.

She is at the end of her second marriage. She has had affairs and gotten caught by her husbands in both cases, and the eventual result has been one divorce and one imminent divorce. She says that as far as her father (whom she adores) is concerned, she is "still a virgin." She wouldn't dream of telling him of the three furtive one-night stands she had with virtual strangers and the one affair that was more than a one-night stand that occurred before her first divorce. She didn't even tell her second husband about that. Neither would she dream of telling Daddy about the three one-night stands and two long-term affairs she has had since about two years after her second marriage began, including the one in which her husband caught her. She had compiled secrets and unfinished business with her father, her first husband, and her current husband.

With my encouragement, she told her husband everything about all her affairs, including the ones since they were married. However, when he didn't get over the news within a month, she started withholding from him again about conversations and meetings she was having with her current male friend. After all, since she doesn't have sex with the friend anymore, there is no need to bring it up, right?

She and her husband don't have sex anymore. She is repulsed by the idea of sex with her husband, but she doesn't want to tell him that because it might hurt his feelings, and she sees no need to do that again. She does meet and have a drink now and then with her former lover and doesn't tell her husband. She feels virtuous for not having sex with her former lover when she talks to him and for "trying to work out" her marriage. She can't understand why in the world I suggest that she clean up her act with her husband again and go and tell her parents everything. It would only hurt and disappoint her father, who is old now and wouldn't understand. She admits that since she told her husband about her previous secret sex life, they have had the best conversations they have ever had, but since he still seems to be deciding to divorce her, she is not sure she believes in this telling the truth stuff.

Linda has plenty of reasons and plenty of social support from her friends to continue to gossip with them and withhold from her husband and not tell her folks about her life, and for God's sake to quit seeing that ridiculous psychologist who is obviously crazy. She is quite pretty and takes good care of her body, even though she suffers from pain caused by being so uptight. She had twice been misdiagnosed as having arthritis before coming to see me, but had flunked the blood tests taken to confirm the diagnosis and confounded several doctors' attempts to figure out what caused her so much pain. She saw no relationship whatsoever between her withholding at the social level and holding back at the physical level to such a degree that all of her joints ached. She did notice, however, that when she cleaned up her withholds with her husband and risked her phony marriage, her pain went away. She got stuck between the rock of going back to the controlled misery of her previous arrangement and "salvaging her marriage," and the hard place of recreating a new marriage based on telling the truth. Worse yet, after starting to hide again from her husband, the damned pain started coming back. My suggestion that she go tell her father the whole story just added to her stress and she started considering finding a more understanding therapist. Because she is so pretty, there are lots of other men out there who are much more understanding than I am anyway, particularly since the subject she needs sympathy about is forgiveness for sex with several men.

From her point of view, she has tried telling the truth at level one and it didn't work because her husband got mad and didn't get over it, so she is not going to make the same mistake with her father or with her husband again. When she reached this conclusion, I suggested that she quit therapy with me. She didn't want to. I set the condition that she tell the truth to her husband and parents at this first level or get out. She got out, still suffering from the stress and physical pain that had brought her to me.

I recommend that people tell the truth because all stress is caused by lying. Some people are too scared to follow through, and others temporarily tell the truth and then go back to lying. If I attempt to do therapy with people who are not willing to take the risk of telling the truth, I am ripping them off. I put up with their withholding and lying for a while and support them to experiment enough to see how it works. About one out of six people leave therapy with me by quitting or getting kicked out.

When I suggest that people clean up their act at the first level and tell their parents, spouses, and friends their long-withheld secrets, they think that's the hardest part. It's not. It is a necessary but not sufficient part of telling the truth. Usually, after resisting for a time and being afraid of the consequences and making a few false starts, people go ahead and come forth with a big withhold to a parent or spouse. Most of the time, parents and siblings can hardly remember, or remember differently, the big trauma and its meaning, or they are not as shocked or righteously indignant or offended or hurt as expected. Usually spouses come forth with withholds of their own and really muddy the water. What happens most is that the anticipated catastrophe doesn't show up — and the client, although greatly relieved, is also a little disappointed. There is a sense of freedom, a gap, a wider sense of being in charge of life, but also a feeling of being nonplussed, like one would feel after having lost a job of some kind.

The new breathing space that is opened up from this first-level work is wonderful, and the client loves me and thinks I am greater than Socrates. Usually I give people a little rest at this place, and we celebrate their newly-renewed relationships. Often I have met the parent or spouse who is the main guarded-against-and-lied-to significant other. Often, in fact, the secrets are revealed in my office and with the aid of my coaching. Usually, instead of being tragic, these sessions are fun. The first level of truth-telling leads to the first level of liberation. You tell *the facts* from the past that have been withheld, you no longer have to be paranoid about being found out, and you get back the energy that was being used up for years to hide the facts. But telling the truth doesn't end with the facts.

Level Two: Honesty About Current Thoughts and Feelings

The second level of telling the truth is to begin to speak forth the emotional truth and the truth of one's judgments — to reveal one's constantly active, secret mind. You begin here the practice of admitting how you feel when you feel it, speaking your secret judgments of others out loud, and constantly revealing your own petty and condescending ways. The first thing people usually think about this next step is: "Oh no, not more!" This is often where people take what psychoanalytic therapists call the "flight into health." They say, "You're a great doctor and a wise person and you have changed my whole life and helped me a lot and I'm eternally grateful, I'm going to split, thank you, goodbye." This response is the mind's attempt to recontrol the situation, take a break and reconceptualize, and take charge of the being again before things get out of hand. The "flight into health" is flight away from a new, scary, but far more effective method of making things happen in the world. Telling the truth creates clearings between yourself and other people where there is a possibility of sharing in creating together. Re-control by the mind's secret, self-protective, judging, hidden self is the attempt to go back to the safer-feeling, hard-earned, adolescent way of being, that worked before and should work again, but leaves you always trying to eat the menu rather than the meal.

The second level of telling the truth, revealing the emotional and judgmental truth on a moment-by-moment basis, is damned hard work and it never ends. Therapy ends, but this work never ends. Therapy ends when the person takes over the task of telling the truth "steady as she goes," as her own task and as her own alternative to manipulation. Manipulating and strategizing and having secret plans and conspiracies is one way to operate in the world to create the appearance of a successful life. But, to recall a previous analogy, the appearance of a successful life is to a successful life as the menu is to a meal. The *appearance* of success is a performance in which you are cut off from contact with the audience except through your role. A successful life, in contrast, is one in which you can share with others openly, as your life happens, without all that rehearsal. The contrast is between performance and sharing. The alternative to telling the simple truth about your feelings and thoughts, as they occur, is a kind of pathetic bragging one is left with in later life even if one has made money — the usual measure of success — but remained an isolated manipulator.

Manipulation *never* works to get the result desired, but it always seems like it's just about to work. When you get what you said you wanted by manipulation, it is never enough. When you tell the truth and get what you want, getting what you want is like gravy — it feels like you are getting more than you ever hoped for, rather than just okay but not quite good enough.

We all get to make this choice between manipulation and communication over and over again in life. John Stevens, a Gestalt educator, wrote beautifully in his book, *Awareness*, about the dilemma of trying to win love through manipulation as opposed to communicating.

> A great deal has been written about trust and love, and that if you can build a trusting, loving relationship, then people can be honest with each other. I believe this idea is exactly backwards. It is very nice if I feel trusting and loving toward someone, but if I don't feel this way, what can I do about it? Trust and love are my *feeling responses* toward another person, and these responses cannot be manufactured. Either I feel love or I don't. All the emphasis on trust and love results in many

people *pretending* to feel trust and love "because it is healthy, and will bring about closeness, honesty, etc." — adding a new area of phoniness and dishonesty in their behavior.

Honesty, however, is a *behavior* and *is* something I can choose or not choose. I cannot decide to love or trust, but I can decide to be personally honest or not. And when I choose to be really honest and say what I experience and what I feel, I am showing that I can be trusted.

≈ ≈ ≈

This is the *only* kind of behavior that can bring about a response of trust. Trust is my response to a person that I know I can believe. Even if I dislike a person, I can trust him if he is honest with me, and I can respect his willingness to be himself honestly.

≈ ≈ ≈

Likewise, honesty does not always bring a response of love, but it is absolutely essential to it. When I am honestly myself, and you respond warmly and with caring, then love exists. If I calculate and put on phony behavior in order to please you, you may love my *behavior,* but you cannot love *me,* because I have hidden my real existence behind this artificial behavior. Even when you love in response to my phony behavior, I cannot really receive your love. It is poisoned by my knowledge that the love is for the image I have created, not for me. I also have to be continually on guard to be sure that I maintain my image so that your love does not disappear. Since I have shut myself off from your love in this way, I will feel more lonely and unloved, and try even more desperately to manipulate myself and you in order to get this love.

In contrast, when I am honestly myself and you respond to me as I am in that moment, I can receive this fully and know the satisfaction of being really related with you. This honest relating is not always joyful or pleasant — it is sometimes sad, sometimes angry, etc. — but it is always *solid* and *real* and *vitally alive.*[1]

This vitality of relationship is, in fact, the love we try so desperately to win. It is only available to people who practice telling the truth.

The second level of telling the truth comes about through experimenting, usually in group therapy as well as in real life, to find out the difference between trying to make things happen through manipulation and having things happen through telling the truth. Once you decide to live that way, you have to continue to work away at it, because the most important thing to know about the truth is that it changes. You can be really mad at someone and hurt by him or her and stay stuck there. Or you can tell them and express it out loud and what was true a moment ago becomes no longer true.

Beth and Mark had both been in therapy with me in the

earlier part of their relationship about 10 years ago. She is 45 years old and he is 29. She is divorced with two grown children. He graduated from college 5 years ago. They relocated twice since he found work after graduating. He lost his job and decided to leave Beth and go live with a younger woman he had met and had a brief affair with. He had told Beth almost everything but was still in a panic of sorts about it all. He came to see me for one visit. I had him go back and talk to Beth and tell her in greater detail everything he had done and everything he appreciated her for and everything he resented her for and all of his thoughts, ideas, and opinions. He did tell her all that he had done. They argued and cried, and then he moved to the city where he planned to seek work and live with his new lover.

Beth kept crying and was really suffering for weeks. She couldn't stop grieving and suffering and hating him for his betrayal and missing him and loving him at the same time.

Finally, having driven a considerable distance to see me, she told me she was trying to keep from thinking about killing herself. She also told me that she and Mark had made a pledge to stay out of contact with each other for 3 months. I thought that was a mistake. I told her to call Mark and have him come to see her so she could tell him her resentments again, her appreciations, judgments, evaluations, and everything she could come up with again and to use the talk with him as an opportunity for her to experience completely the feelings she had and let them go away. I recommended that instead of avoiding and waiting to see what happened if they stayed apart, that they get together and let the past die. I told her to get a mediator and gave her the name of a therapist in the town where she lived. (I told her to get the mediator to make sure she completed the job.) She left to go home for Thanksgiving, having decided to face the music.

A few days later, we got this letter from Beth:

November 27, Sunday night

Dearest Brad and Amy,

Mark left about 30 minutes ago, and I want to let you know that all is fine. Brad, for the first time in my life, I didn't do what you said; I didn't get a mediator; I didn't even try. I found I didn't need it, and I was more comfortable with the idea of not having one.

Mark arrived here about 11:15 this morning and stayed until 5:30. I knew when he walked in the door that he wasn't going to stonewall me. The first thing I said was, "May I give you a hug?" He said yes, and we hugged for a long moment. Then we sat down and talked and talked. After a while — actually a long while — I fixed us some dinner, and we ate and talked some more.

He cried a lot and I cried some. I told him all the things I wanted to say — all the resentments and all the appreciations. At this point, all of the resentments turned out to be appreciations, anyway, which is always a miracle to me when it happens. I said I was glad he had left and glad I had been precipitated into crisis, because I wouldn't have missed doing this for anything in the world. I had needed to do a lot of this, and had never done it, and now I have. At least, I've started. He said he hadn't allowed himself to grieve much at all.

He told me that he still loved me, too, and that he had missed me in every room of the house and everywhere he had been and all the time. I said that I cherished the love I have for him, and that what was left was for me to become detached from him, and that I was on my way to doing that. I really don't believe that I left anything unsaid that I needed to say, and if I did, I'll have a chance to say it another time. We're going to keep in touch, and he asked if he could come back when he was ready to talk about himself. Mostly today what he did was have very strong grief reactions and sadness to what I said to him.

At one point, we held each other and kissed and I told him I appreciated him for doing that, because it was the first time I had felt horny since he had walked out the door, and I hadn't been sure I still had that reaction in me.

Eventually we made love and beautifully and really good, and I was glad for that, and didn't feel as if I couldn't bear to let him go. If that makes any sense.

You were right, Brad, in that I did find that Mark is not as evil as I had believed and a lot more desperate than I had thought. And it's not my problem anymore. I told him I'd be as good a friend to him as I could, and that I couldn't rescue him. I had tried, and it just hadn't worked.

I had, by the way, a perfectly wonderful Thanksgiving. My sister was here, and her son, and, of course, Mother, and we had a great dinner and a lot of laughing and talking. I found ever since Tuesday, that I can laugh with my whole self again. And I can still be sad and miss Mark and hate thinking about Christmas without him. And I am just a little relieved that I have had those reactions, since I believe I would be just a bit strange not to have them.

Since I started sorting out what was going on with me, I've found some patterns of behavior in me that I didn't recognize before — like what a controlling person I've been, for one. And the classic caretaker-type person, obsessed with the behavior of someone else. And I've found that I probably have another big problem to work on — and I don't know in the slightest how to start, although I imagine I'll get to it eventually. That is, being a non-achiever. I wouldn't even classify myself as an underachiever. There's bound to be some pattern I learned somewhere along the way that I bought into.

Anyway, that's where I am. And I send loads of love to you both for the part you played in my gaining insight with which to work, and the push I needed to plunge myself into the depths of despair and horror in order to get out of it. And, above all, I love you both for the love and support you showed me. Another thing that's come out of this is the knowledge that I have more friends than I knew I had, and most of them care enough to tell the truth, at least as far as they can see it, and for some it's pretty far.

Much, much love,
Beth

Beth cured her incessant grieving by contact and open conversation with Mark. When incessant grieving occurs, it is usually out of the person's attempt to handle *anger* by *crying* and feeling bad and having obsessional thoughts. Once the resentment and appreciation and hurt get sorted out and expressed, the grieving subsides enough for the person to make a new start. The person forgives her lover, not for the lover's benefit but for her own. She experiences the love, and lets go. She experiences the hatred, and lets go. Finally, she experiences the grief and lets go. In the process she forgives herself, *because in that deeper self, formed back when she was a very small child, she felt like anything bad that happened was really her fault.* So in the process of getting into and getting over rotten feelings about others, we get over the rotten feelings about ourselves. Through the process of forgiving our enemies our own forgiveness occurs. This is why we have to forgive others: *for our own benefit.* Beth forgave Mark and herself. Then she stopped taking care of him by protecting him from the truth of her anger and her love and her notions about him.

Mark was another story. Because he felt guilty for having hurt her by running off with another woman, and a younger one at that, he couldn't add insult to injury, so he never allowed himself to get mad at her. He was desperate over having lost his job and his former relationship (two roles in which he had felt safe, though also trapped for a long time). A few months later he killed himself in his new girl friend's apartment. His anger, never sufficiently expressed, his fear, never sufficiently acknowledged, his judgments, never sufficiently exposed to another, wore him out and his mind ate him. He had told the truth about what he had been hiding from Beth at level one, but he held back on sharing his feelings with anyone during this time of great stress and distress.

He engineered his suicide with great skill and deliberation. His mind was thorough and efficient. Only his relatedness was impaired. He used his mind to kill himself to escape his mind.

When a person has not sufficiently expressed himself by telling the truth at this second level, the mind makes assessments. These judgments are distorted by the emotions withheld and avoided. Judgments like, "I'm too tired," "I can't take it anymore," "It's not worth the struggle," and "I've got to get out of this place," are products of incomplete disclosure of feelings toward, and thoughts about, others. Beth, unlike Mark, achieved deliverance from her mind's tyranny by telling the truth at the second level. Both started with similar suffering. He died, literally, by his own hand. She died to who she had been and achieved transformation. Who she was to herself passed away, and she moved on. The government of the early formative mind was overthrown and no longer dominated the being. This transformation is as powerful as the reverse is tragic.

The following excerpts from D.H. Lawrence's poem, *A New Heaven and a New Earth*, celebrate this type of liberation.

I was so weary of the world.
I was so sick of it.
everything was tainted with myself,
skies, trees, flowers, birds, water,
people, houses, streets, vehicles, machines,
nations, armies, war, peace-talking,
work, recreation, governing, anarchy,
it was all tainted with myself, I knew it all to start with
because it was all myself.

When I gathered flowers, I knew it was myself plucking my
own flowering,
When I went on a train, I knew it was myself travelling by
my own invention.
When I heard the canon of the war, I listened with my own
ears to my own destruction.
When I saw the torn dead, I knew it was my own torn dead
body.
It was all me. I had done it all in my own flesh.

I shall never forget the maniacal horror of it all in the end
when everything was me, I knew it all already, I anticipated
it all in my soul.

because I was the author and the result
I was the God and the creation at once;
creator, I looked at my creation;
created, I looked at myself, the creator;
it was a maniacal horror in the end.

෴ ෴ ෴

At last came death, sufficiency of death,
and that at last relieved me, I died.

෴ ෴ ෴

and I am dead, and trodden to nought in the smoke sodden
tomb;
dead and trodden to nought in the sour black earth
of the tomb; dead and trodden to nought, trodden to nought.

God, but it is good to have died and been trodden out,
trodden to nought in sour, dead earth,
quite to nought,
absolutely to nothing
nothing
nothing
nothing.

For when it is quite, quite nothing, then it is everything.
When I am trodden quite out, quite, quite out,
every vestige gone, then I am here
risen, accomplishing a resurrection
risen, not born again, but risen, body the same as before,
new beyond knowledge of newness, alive beyond life,

proud beyond inkling or furthest conception of pride,
living where life was never yet dreamed of, nor hinted at,
here, in the other world, still terrestrial
myself, the same as before, yet unaccountably new.

I, in the sour black tomb, trodden to absolute death
I put out my hand in the night, one night, and my hand
touched that which was verily not me,
verily it was not me.
Where I had been was a sudden blaze,
a sudden flaring blaze!
So I put my hand out further, a little further
and I felt that which was not I,
it verily was not I,
it was the unknown.

Ha, I was a blaze leaping up!
I was a tiger bursting into sunlight.
I was greedy, I was mad for the unknown.
I, new risen, resurrected, starved from the tomb,
starved from a life of devouring always myself,
now here was I, new awakened, with my hand stretching
out
and touching the unknown, the real unknown, the unknown
unknown.

My God, but I can only say
I touch, I feel the unknown!

[83]

I am the first comer!
Cortes, Pisarro, Columbus, Cabot, they are nothing,
nothing!
I am the first comer!
I am the discoverer!
I have found the other world!

It was the flank of my wife
I touched with my hand, I clutched with my hand,
rising, new awakened from the tomb!
It was the flank of my wife
whom I married years ago
at whose side I have lain for over a thousand nights
and all that previous while, she was I, she was I;
I touched her, it was I who touched and I who was touched.

Yet rising from the tomb, from the black oblivion
stretching out my hand, my hand flung like a drowned man's
hand on a rock,
I touched her flank and knew I was carried by the current in
death
over to the new world, and I was climbing out on the shore,
risen, not to the old world, the old, changeless I, the old life,
wakened not to the old knowledge
but to a new earth, a new I, a new knowledge, a new world
of time.[2]

The utter and complete newness, the vitality of original experience that Lawrence celebrates here, is available only through the destruction of the old world of lies, roles, and secrets. The death of this tainted world is the rebirth of the *authentic* self, including the world and the relationships that partly constitute that self.

Level Three: Exposing the Fiction

Imagine living out of the transformation D.H. Lawrence describes! This is the third level of telling the truth: the place where telling the truth and living the truth become the same. This is the place of which the Hindus say, "If you speak the truth long enough, your word becomes universal law." The third level of telling the truth occurs when *you admit that who you are is not who you have been pretending to be.* What you have been selling other people on, and selling yourself on, is not who you are. You don't really know who you are. You confess disillusionment with beliefs you used to stand for, and various sales pitches you did and still do for your act. This is at first embarrassing, then for a while something to brag about, and then just a description of what happened to you in the course of growing up.

The process of demythologizing yourself is begun by bragging about all the things which, in your false modesty, you were pretending you didn't care about. You have to go through your vanity and the suffering associated with it. You have to show off and be embarrassed, both of which are egotism, and you can't skip, dodge, or get around this step. You have to praise yourself openly rather than manipulate to suck praise. You have to acknowledge being a secret hero to yourself and confess the putrid vanity of all of your usual phony self-denigration. You have to admit what a worm and a liar you are and go through the feelings that come up when you tell the truth about all of this. If you have never truly embarrassed yourself by what you had to say about yourself, you don't know shit from shinola about transformation. When you get to telling the truth about all of it, you are at level three. Who you are becomes more a description centered in the here and now, and less of a story about your life.

When you admit your act you also admit your ignorance. You confess that you developed your act in order not to appear lost and in hopes of finding your way by faking it. Then you admit that you are lost and faking it most of the time these days as well, not just in the far-removed past. Before you acted smart; now you acknowledge ignorance like it is gold.

I conduct a nine-day workshop several times every year. One of the exercises we do involves telling the entire story of our life to the group while being videotaped, answering everyone's questions, and then watching the tape. People demonstrate their attachment to various times in their lives and are moved at the places kept precious to memory. The most-remembered times are usually the hard times, and the person whose story it is turns out to be a hero or heroine in spite of difficult or unfair circumstances. Usually, the younger a person is, the longer it takes them to tell their story. Younger people (in their 20s) seem to have more significant moments in which details and interpretations of meaning are very important. It is this ego-attachment to having heroically survived the unfairness of the world that has to be given up at level three of telling the truth. This is a breakthrough to the newness and innocence of young awareness, after you have been adolescent, mind-bound, and jaded for years.

Nobody I know stays at level three constantly. Continuous waves of freedom and new egotism, one liberation after another, keep just getting you back to the same place. But if you are in a community which supports you in telling the truth, you get to level three more often.

Level three is sharing with other people in ways that occasionally allow you to overcome your own egotism, including the egotism that comes from thinking you are great for telling the truth. You start considering yourself to be a person who attained level three. You have attained, in fact, a higher level than most people, grown further than most people, and you are proud of yourself. You know that your act is not who you are, just a useful development that came from growing up.

You have been good. You've grown a long way. You have admitted not knowing how to find your ass with both hands with some embarrassment and you deserve a reward. "I'm great, I am a superior being, good for me, this is it, I've growed up, I've attained enlightenment and I am special," you say to yourself. Your hard-earned humility is quickly followed by pride in your humility.

Owning up to the fact that there is no virtue in owning up is the continuation of the third level of telling the truth. What you end up with if you drop your new pride is innocence much like you had before you developed an identity. What you have then is an identity without being much attached to it.

There is less to learn at the third level of telling the truth, but it takes more work and practice than other levels. This level involves practice more than insight. It's like the difference between being a good amateur golfer and becoming a professional in the game. There is a lot of fine tuning of skills and practice to keep them sharp, and it takes longer than the other three levels generally take. As far as I know, it is never over.

My expertise is at an end here. Not that expertise has ever helped a hell of a lot at earlier levels, but I have had more experience there. To concentrate on things outside of your reputation to yourself doesn't require any effort at all, so it is hard as hell to do. Our minds are always working. This ceaseless mental activity will continue to occur whether we take it seriously or not. But the practice of taking it less seriously can't be taken too seriously or we are back in our minds again. The less credence we give to our minds' ongoing activity, the more we detach from identifying with that activity, the less it wears us out. Level three involves vigilance against being taken over by the mind. You never get a break. There is no reward to it except clarity and a little less strain. What is true changes, so we can't tell the truth once and be done with it. It's an ongoing game.

Life is a game in which the rules change as the game progresses, and you have to know where you are in the game to know what rules to play by. Furthermore, you can't ever be certain where you are in the game, and the rules don't always apply.

Learning to Tell the Truth is like Learning to Play Golf
When you learn golf at the first level you practice the fundamentals until you can hit the ball. At the second level, you polish up

your basic skills and lower your score by playing a lot. The third level involves admitting that thinking about your experience and wisdom about golf and 65 cents will get you a cup of coffee, that stories you have and tell about great golf shots or even great golf rounds are just bullshit about golf and not the same as playing golf. When you've got that, you actually start getting better, and you start dreaming of becoming a par golfer. When you start beating the people who used to beat you, and beat your teacher, you are solidly at the third level, because if you were thinking about beating them while you were actually playing you wouldn't have beat them. You learn that each shot has nothing to do with the last, or with your reputation for good shots at any preceding point.

The third level, becoming a professional, is the hardest. To move from good to professional is harder than any of the other advances, even though we're just talking about changing an average score for 18 holes by a few strokes. To go from "good" to professional is tougher than getting from unskilled to good.

Each level of advancement takes more work. At the last level, even though the difference in score is very slight, the difference in playing ability is immense. It takes a long time and an unusual amount of dedication to move from a high level of skill to a higher level. A lot of people go for it and don't make it, in golf and tennis and a lot of other sports.

Daydreaming about being a pro can interfere with your practice and your game. Planning each shot and then being present to the shot you are making over and over again is a level of non-hysterical concentration in which the ego of the concentrator doesn't exist because there is no difference in that being concentrated on and the concentrator — no difference between the act and the actor, the play and the player. The ball is hit and it rolls towards the hole and you wonder why people want to give you credit for it.

To really clean up your act with regard to lying is like becoming a pro. If you were well-loved as a small child, you have more natural ability for the first level of growth in telling the truth. If you suffered a lot in developing your identity in adolescence, but developed an identity that showed forth regardless of the roles you played, so that the lies you told yourself and others about who you were actually worked, you have a better chance of making it past the second level of telling the truth.

You have to have an ego to give one up. You can only admit the truth about your various poses, and your fundamental pose (what many personality theorists call the self), after you have developed a fundamental pose that works and serves you well. Then, you can become dissatisfied with the limitations imposed by that pose.

At level three, you have to get over your new egotism about having made it to level three. Once you come off it two or three times and admit your pretentiousness, and you get to thinking you are pretty virtuous, you must then own up to the fact that owning up to the facts is not a virtue, just growth. There is great despair associated with that. Getting into that despair leads directly to the here-and-now self. The work is analogous to becoming the best amateur golfer and winning a couple of amateur tournaments and deciding to become a pro. You work and work and work and finally give up. Then, once you have lost hope, if you keep playing, you're a pro.

Understanding telling the truth, like understanding golf, is relatively simple. Doing it is a little harder. Still, it's clear that the revelations at each level of telling the truth allow for greater sharing of who a person is and what they are about. When we reveal more, we have less to hide. When we have less to hide, we are less worried about being found out. When we are less worried about being found out, we can pay better attention to someone else. In this way, telling the truth makes intimacy and freedom possible.

Now, since I am supposed to be a pro at this, let me tell you more about who I am and what I am about and we'll see if I cover all the levels.

The Truth About Why I am Writing This Book

I am writing this book because I want to become famous. I want a lot of people to know my name, now and after I die. I want to be known as a great intellect, and perceiver, and I want to be smarter than anyone else. More precisely, I want to be thought to be smarter than everyone else. The pleasure of imagining other people imagining me smarter is an experience of warmth, a dull but pleasant sensation accompanied by a slight smile and an inner vision of people reading my book and talking about me with excitement, like my wife Amy and I do reading Friedrich Nietzsche, who is long dead.

The pleasure of fantasizing about the future is hard to describe. It is a lot like being really wrapped up in a novel or being so into a task that an enjoyable experience of forgetting about time occurs. It is enjoyable mostly because I am not worrying at the time. Fantasy about the future takes the place of worry, and the feeling is pleasant rather than straining. This fantasy about becoming famous has a lot of related fantasies that are also pleasurable. For example, this morning I had the fantasy that a TV interviewer was interviewing me on camera about this book. He asked some TV-morning-show type of stupid question, so I refused to answer and began questioning him. I said, "Why do you ask such stupid questions?" I love to imagine putting down one of those dumb-assed interviewers on the morning talk shows for their snivelling, simpy ways, pushing people to hurry up and say something. I hate morning shows and *Time* magazine and all the hysterical assholes who work for them. I hate a lot of the stupid people I see on television every day and I like hating them. I love hating them. I love hating them because it makes me certain that although I may be bad, I am not as fucked up as those people.

What a pleasure it is to have a fantasy of malice! When I have the fantasy, I experience energy in my body that is pleasurable to me. I like fantasies of righteous anger. My heart speeds up and I get a hit of energy. It's exciting, like listening to the Lone Ranger on the radio when I was in grade school. The fantasies that invigorate me, that evoke this excitement, are a constant source of entertainment to me.

I want to become famous. I am pissed. I get pleasure by imagining myself being more right and powerful than you other assholes. I want to prove that I'm better than you at telling the truth by teaching you how to do it. Hardly anyone knows the value of telling the truth — so it looks like an opportune opening to make a reputation for myself.

I also want to be a good man. I want to help people. I imagine myself as the savior. I get off on imagining me saving you from the ravages of your own mind. I get quite a good hit of my own energy from that fantasy.

I write this book to warm myself with fantasies. Some of my favorite fantasies are fame, righteous anger, superiority, power, and being a savior. I imagine I want to save everyone. I want to save the whole world. I like to think of myself as helping to save the world. I think I *am* helping to save the world. I like the work. I believe that evoking feeling as opposed to suppressing feeling will open an opportunity to save the world. I enjoy imagining myself a leader in encouraging people to live out loud, to reveal what is hidden, to tell the truth and let the chips fall where they may. I like to think of myself as a good man for getting people to adopt this as a life stance from the beginning — as a stand to take in the world. Jesus was a good angry man who wanted to save the world. I want to be like Jesus.

I want to make money from writing this book. I want to have a lot of people wanting to come see me in therapy or be in one of my groups or come to my "Telling the Truth" workshops. I want to get rich so I can travel and write more. I am already rich but I'm greedy and I want more than most people have. I'm like Judas in that way. I want just a little extra.

I also want to write this book in support of people who have been in therapy with me and people who have been with other therapists like me. I want to speak to friends who have grown up with me, some of whom I know and some I don't know. I feel virtuous and proud to be the kind of guy I am.

Finally, I write to clarify my own thoughts because I think my thoughts are important. When I have to perform like this, for a while, my life has meaning and clarity. That I have these fantasies, thoughts, and poses is the truth. I am not just playing like they are true to demonstrate my ideas about the levels of telling the truth. I want these things, and I think these things and masturbate my frontal lobes with these things.

So, I want to become famous. I am pissed. I want to be a good man. I want to make money. I want to support people. I want to think clearly. That about covers it.

These things I want are also false, they are lies, they don't exist, they are bullshit. The fantasies make me feel good. I tell you my fantasies and some of them make you think I'm a good person and some make you think I am a bad person, but they all are calculated to make you think I am an exceptional person. If I lie to you in order to make you think I am really an exceptionally good person, and you buy it, maybe I can convince myself. The only trouble is, I know the bastard who was doing the sales pitch in the first place.

What could keep me trapped at this level would be withholding fantasy on the basis of fantasy, like if I didn't tell you the truth about my "delusions of grandeur" so you wouldn't think I was an asshole and not buy my book. But I also know that if you are looking for a book that wasn't written by an asshole you've got a long search ahead of you. Every asshole who writes a book is a neurotic megalomaniac just like me. Most other writers have enough sense to withhold fantasies on the basis of another fantasy that it is politic to withhold fantasies. Most writers are trapped in their minds.

You are "politic" in this way when you imagine yourself a good person because you don't tell your wife about jacking off while thinking about her sister, or don't tell your boss about your secret plans, or don't tell your mother you pissed in the chicken soup when you were 12. This is being so lost in illusion you can't possibly ever reach young adulthood. Tell your wife the truth about your fantasies about everyone else, including her sister (and all those animals and things, too); tell your boss about your plans, your mistakes, and all that marijuana you smoked; and for God's sake, tell your mother about the soup. If the truth is told you'll feel relieved, because you have been *anxious* in some vague way for so long you forgot where it came from, but kept it up anyway, because you knew something bad was about to happen but just couldn't remember what it was. Anxiety is what accompanies fantasy crashes and near-collisions.

Depression is the state accompanying gridlock in fantasyland. Most of us daydream a while and play in the world a while in just the way I have described, the time spent in the daydreams being much greater. *Learning to balance consciously the daydreaming and living requires a clear distinction between lying and the truth.* What clears the space for that distinction is getting to where you don't care what anyone knows about you. Fuck 'em if they can't take a joke.

I write this book out of a daydream of power and to work on the pleasure of thinking and brooding and to burn a few illusions to warm myself with and to create an imagined future that won't be what I had hoped for when it gets here. It is more fun to share and produce and create out of fantasy than to withhold out of fantasy. Not to tell you of my dreams of fame and power and money might help me protect my pose as an expert and keep you from thinking just another jerk wrote this book. But just another jerk did write this book.

Who Do You Think *You* Are ?
Detachment from the goals, projects, and evaluations of the mind is accomplished through a change in how we identify who we are. The purpose of telling the truth at all levels is to disconnect from and step back from previous identities.

When we identify the electric-perceiver-being-of-the-moment as who we are, the being like a six-month-old child — alive, alert, and not trapped in preconception — we locate and anchor in present-tense experience. When this occurs, we gain the power to use our minds as tools rather than as machines for the defense of who we think we ought to have other people think we are.

Most of us, most of the time, identify ourselves as our case histories and become embroiled in the dilemmas of the mind. By paying attention to the language people use, I can tell whether they are identifying with the "case-history-and-judge" self or the "being-in-the-moment" self. The language of the "being-in-the-moment" self is the language of the Lone Ranger's friend Tonto: "Me hungry." "Me thirsty." "Me wanta go."

When therapy works to relieve anxiety or depression or delusional pain, there is a transformation of the way life is *because of a change in who a person says he is.* Therapy is not merely to modify the behavior of the case-history self. Therapy has worked when the subject's whole identification with his case history is loosened, and an identification with his self-in-the-moment predominates. When this happens, people talk differently.

Of course, successful therapy does radically modify the behavior one would predict based on the case history. These modifications are a secondary effect of transformation. They are the result of the subject's owning and using the case-history self from the standpoint of identification with the being-in-the-moment self. You identify yourself as that light of attention that is on in this moment and was on in those past moments. Those past moments are merely records that exist in this moment and that's all they are. Who you were before this second is already dead. Who you are is merely who you are now, memory included, heartbeat of time included, now dead again, now born again, now dead again, again.

You see, all that I just said about myself is true. All of what I just said about myself is also a joke. All of what I just said about myself is just a memory, kept alive for a few seconds again so I can feel consistent about who I think I am.

Getting born again feels real good for a while, until we get to thinking that who we are is someone who got born again. That someone who got born again needs to die again, and get born again, again. And so forth.

I pretend on the one hand to be an authority, and on the other to have no authority. Both claims are true. And who I am right now doesn't have much to do with the evaluations and judgments that make up the role of authority, or the role of authority who simultaneously claims no authority. These poses are meaningless. The value of acknowledging these meaningless poses is that the limitations they impose on my way of being are lifted. I may still use what I know and admit what I don't know without worrying about what it means about me. The value of getting free from role domination is greater energy to use for creation rather than defense.

Who You Are

What you are looking at now is a piece of paper with ink on it. Who you are is the one looking. That being you are, looking at the page, is the one to surrender your case-history self to. That being you are, looking at this page now, is the greater context within which your case-history personality resides. Who *you* are is a unique version of the holy human prototype, with personality included. ⌒

III

*Liberation of the Being
from its Mind*

BEING ABNORMALLY HONEST

"I ought to go upright and vital,
and speak the rude truth in all ways."
— Ralph Waldo Emerson

WHEN THE *being*, for whom the light first came on in the womb and who is the background aliveness run by the involuntary nervous system, speaks, it uses a particular language. The *mind*, which grew out of the being like trees grow out of the earth, is at first a protector of being and after a while becomes a parasite. When the *mind* speaks, it also uses a particular language. The language of the being is *descriptive* language. The language of the mind is *evaluative* language.

When you tell the truth, you are free simply by virtue of describing what is so. This descriptive language evokes a feeling of affirmation, a willingness to be, an appreciation for being alive in the world as it is. When someone speaks the truth everyone around them is touched and there is hardly anything to say back except, "Ain't it the truth." The being within which the mind resides is then speaking and is in charge of the mind rather than getting used by the mind.

The secret of the good life is not suffocating in the mind's bullshit. Bullshit is like heroin (or a warm blanket or money in the bank or life insurance) — it feels so good and protected and safe and warm that even if you *do* choke on your own puke, you don't mind so much. The alternative, freedom, is often too terrifying for a mind to tolerate, so the mind hides from freedom behind piles of bullshit, under blankets of evaluation, in a bed of memories. Describing what is true ruins the escape from freedom that being lost in the mind offers. Descriptive words come out of beings who are in charge of their minds. Evaluative language comes out of minds in charge of being. People who speak simply and clearly have chosen freedom over the escape into the illusion of security.

Freedom, the Language of Freedom, the Feeling of Freedom
An honest person is free by virtue of not being lost in her own mind. An honest person is a being within whom the ongoing flow of experience occurs, and who has a mind full of guiding abstractions, but for whom neither circumstance nor principles *dictate* action. Action that is clearly intentional occurs, but results from consciousness of circumstance, of principles, and of consciousness itself. The simple language that points to experience, as well as language that summarizes and abstracts from experience, are both spoken by the honest person. The unitary background principle is not the level of abstraction, but the intention to accurately describe what is so, regardless of considerations of propriety. When I speak clearly, I experience movement and sensation in my body and evoke the same in the body of the person spoken

to. When they speak back clearly, we both are moved again. Honest people are continually surprised by unexpected sensation and movement, and have learned not to mind that so much. The time comes when the feeling of insecurity becomes less than a dreaded occurrence. It becomes a most precious and valued form of excitement, a way of experiencing being alive in a heightened way, a way of getting high. Most of us never overcome the butchering of our upbringing enough to discover how to tolerate the experience of freedom and learn to relish having it.

Words Are Labels for Pictures, and None of Them Are Real
About a dozen times in the past fifteen years, I have gone to Greece, to the Island of Patmos, which I particularly love. Every time I go back, I strike out walking across the hills, looking at the sea and the other islands in the distance and the blue sky, saying over and over to myself in my mind, "Damn, I'm glad to be back! I am back again! This is just like before. It's as beautiful as ever! This sure is beautiful!" After I walk a while, I begin to settle down, and I start talking to myself in a different way. "Those are just rocks. That is just dirt. That is just water. Those are just other islands." After some time of this, it occurs to me, "How beautiful this is!" It seems to come out of the sea and the light and the sky and the land. The word "beautiful" seems to describe an experience that occurs out of being there in that moment. When I was using the word earlier, it came out of my memories, making comparisons with other times and places. It was a reiteration of something I already knew. The first "beautiful" was from my mind. The second came from my experience, and my mind described it.

A word is only a *label* for a *picture* of something real. A word or short phrase is only a caption for a remembered snapshot of a real thing, not the real thing that is here right now. That may seem unimportant or self-evident, but it turns out to make a lot of difference in who you think you are.

You can perceive many more colors with your senses than you can report with the language of description. So many tones of each color exist that only a kind of gross "pointing to" occurs with the words "red," "pink," "blue," etc. There is a time in the evenings right after sunset when ultra-violet light transforms greens to super-greens and colors the colors one tone more. This time provokes in me an eerie feeling that accompanies the heightened color perception. I love walking at sunset, but it makes me a little sad. The "blues" I have in the evening, deep and sad and full of love and a sense of passing away, can't be evoked by language so much as by evening itself. When I attempt to speak to you of feelings within my own being it is hard to know what you get from what I say. I have enough difficulty describing the tones of color or sound or warmth or other sensations, so when I attempt to share feelings within me, evoked by some already indescribable evening, the task is even harder. Language may be inadequate to the task of complete communication.

Sometimes when we make love we think and feel that a communication deeper than language occurs. But how can you tell? There is no way to verify this connection except with language that can't quite express what I be like, or you be like, when we be making love. There have been times when I thought sex was incredible and I was sure my partner particularly enjoyed it and I asked and she said she thought it was okay but not the best. The reverse has also happened.

Telling the truth is hard enough if all we mean by it is communicating what events occur, without even trying to communicate about our feelings. When we are watching a sunset with another person we can always just point to the sunset and keep our mouths shut and assume we are communicating both about the experience and our evaluation of the experience. When there is no sunset to point to, one has to be particularly concerned with language. e.e. cummings says that a poet is someone who is "abnormally fond of that precision which creates movement."[1] I say this is true of an honest person. Being descriptive of one's own feelings in so precise a way as to evoke feeling in another is the heart of the creative power of poetry and of honest speech. But feelings and thoughts are more difficult to tell the truth about than events. All words are abstractions. Although words that have immediate referents in the world are less abstract than words that cover a lot of territory, speak of general feelings, or make global assessments, they are still not the *thing described.* Words can "point to" something in the world like a chair, or something in a person like a feeling. When one is totally committed and captivated by pointing to what is so, one finds words to speak the truth, regardless of the level of abstraction.

Abstractions are a part of what is so. Feelings associated with abstractions are a part of what is so. You can still tell the truth by "pointing to" an abstraction or assessment of your mind, if your intent is simply to point out your thought, rather than to make the other person believe your thought to be the "right interpretation" of reality. This is the difference between sharing and a sales pitch. When thoughts and feelings are shared in this way, *you get the benefit of the correction or modification of your mind's view of reality* that can only come when you put your thoughts out there in the public domain.

In an introduction to a book of poems, e.e. cummings has this to say:

"It is with roses and locomotives (not to mention acrobats Spring electricity Coney Island the 4th of July the eyes of mice and Niagara Falls) that my 'poems' are competing.

"They are also competing with each other, with elephants, and with El Greco."[2]

He has had his attention wholly captured in the highest form of concentration possible: fascination. Being completely given over to these experiences allowed him to create the sentence that compared them with each other. To report on the electrifying experience of being with exemplary instances of aliveness awakens us to the truth of experience.

My experiences of being present to a child's laughter, a sunset, the eyes of mice, and Niagara Falls are records in my mind that can be re-evoked by language that points to these magnificent events. Somehow when language brings them together it almost outdoes the events. e.e. cummings uses language first to evoke the recollection of the experiences themselves and second, through putting together the recollections, evokes an experience of the combined evoked experiences. The whole of them together are a compilation of magnificence. I am moved not only by the experience, but also by the magnificence of the being who perceives them as alike in wonderment. I love e.e. cummings for his words. I love me through loving him through loving his words. I love all of us magnificent beings for the magnificence of being beings who can appreciate the magnificence of being.

e.e. cummings was a man who was interested in the truth. I am interested in the truth. I know that you are interested in the truth. I know that all of us are. I am interested in the truth of humans being. So are you. I am interested in the ways we attempt to communicate the truth of our human being. So are you. I am eternally frustrated by the limits of language as well as fascinated by the freedom from the mind-jail language can sometimes provide.

Language has the power to evoke the being of human beings and rescue them from their own minds. Skill in the use of this kind of language develops through the practice of telling the truth. The clearer I am willing to be about myself, the more clearly I can see others and the more clearly I can speak to them. You too.

An honest person prefers language that reveals what is so, whether it's about someone else, the world, or himself. Being fascinated with uncovering the truth from a nest of evaluations is the best game in town. It only becomes fun after meaning becomes less serious and pretending has become boring. Going back to putting on a show is a bigger drag than having all be known. Playing in a world where all is known is more challenging and less trivial and less wearing. Letting up on oneself about having to hide and pretend is freeing and it feels good, like breathing fresh air.

Only willingness to hew close to the truth, like some gritty old populist newspaper editor, wins through to the liberation that comes from telling the truth. It's almost impossible to do without great commitment. It can, however, be done, even by the most mind-ravaged people, if they have the support of other people who are also committed to telling the truth.

Telling the Truth Sucks

Telling the truth means all of the worst things you might imagine it means. It means telling everything you have hidden that you have done in the past to the very people who you think would be most hurt or angry or surprised or embarrassed by the revelations. If, for example, you have been having sex with someone other than your spouse, you have to tell him/her all the details: who you did it with, how many times, who came first, how many times you came, where it happened, who you told, what you said to each other, how much fun it was, and so on, and answer all the questions that arise from the telling. Telling the truth means telling all your secrets and your secret feelings to whomever you don't want to tell. Worse yet, it means being expressive of feeling — mad when you express resentment and warm and moved when you express appreciation and silent when you don't yet know what you feel. Telling the truth has to do with being expressive of feeling and using descriptive language regardless of ideas about tact or propriety. The first thing you have to get over to tell the truth is politeness — modification of your report of your experience out of "consideration" of the other person's feelings. That is, unless your spouse gets a clear feeling from your report of how much fun it was when you fucked her best friend, you haven't told the truth yet.

Honest people speak simply, using language more to *describe* than to *evaluate*. Liars evaluate almost exclusively, only using enough description to make the story believable. Good liars use a little more description than bad liars, more subtle in its cast of value so the listener thinks she came up with the idea about whether what happened was good or bad. Hours and hours of practice and observation have helped us all in developing our ability to manipulate in this way. We all have a sales pitch about the nature of reality.

When a person chooses to make the transition from habitual lying to telling the truth, the passage is scary and difficult. We have learned to assign value dishonestly and pitch our point of view with everything we say. We have been trained by scores of moralistic authorities, like Nurse Ratchet in Ken Kesey's *One Flew Over the Cuckoo's Nest*, to keep our mouths shut and behave as we should instead of speaking the truth. We have been blackmailed into a common interpretation of reality by hundreds of male and female Nurse Ratchets. Learning to *describe*, to speak what is simply true, requires an unlearning of hard-earned preconceptions and a relearning of how to perceive with as little preconception as possible.

Knowing the difference between perception and *con*ception and getting good, through practice, at distinguishing between the two can save your life. Both the quality and length of your life can be increased through learning to focus on making the distinction over and over again between value-laden words and descriptive words.

Descriptive words make pictures happen in the mind of the speaker and the hearer, create experiences like smells, sexual excitement, anger, righteous indignation, embarrassment, sympathy, sadness, joyfulness, or laughter. An honest person is one who is creating vivid pictures, feelings, sounds, and smells in the singular attempt to portray what has occurred or is occurring within her or around her. An honest person is concerned foremost with accuracy. Being honest is not just for the sake of feeling good about being a virtuous person; it is a vital necessity. *Learning how to be honest and being willing to do so is the cure for all non-environmental stress disorders.* It is the key to managing the disease of moralism. It is the most worthwhile focus of our attention as humans of this time and the only thing with half a chance to save us from ourselves. This is vital to our life and to the survival of life for all of us.

Our problems do not arise from not thinking enough before we speak. Just the opposite is true. The way we learn to think and modify what we have to say before we speak kills millions of us unnecessarily and lays waste most of the cripples left, injured but still alive.

In the Centers for Disease Control study referred to in the introduction, the list of causes of deaths in individuals under age 65 goes like this: environment is responsible for 21 percent of deaths; the health care system for nine percent; and human biology for 17 percent. Think about that. Twenty-one percent of the people who die before age 65 are killed by war, traffic, accidents, acts of God, and crime. Nine percent get killed by doctors, nurses, hospitals, and medicine. In 17 percent of the cases, the human biological machine breaks in some way that is not blamable on the way the people took care of themselves. *That means the remaining 53 percent of the deaths prior to age 65 come about as a result of the way people choose to live their lives.*

I believe the ways we take care of ourselves so poorly arise out of the starvation we experience from being cut off from the nourishment of commonplace experience, including the experience of intimacy. We are responsible for cutting ourselves off from experience by substituting our interpretations of reality for reality. We invent some fundamental lies about how life should be and shouldn't be, how life is or isn't according to what we have taught ourselves to ignore or deny and what can or cannot be talked about. We compensate for our sense of something missing and our boredom with a kind of frenetic, compulsive use of food, alcohol, and drugs to try to get temporary relief from imprisonment in our own minds.

We are all terrible liars. People with notable stress disorders like ulcers, insomnia, spastic colitis, etc., are worse liars than normal people, although normal people are generally unhappy from lying, withholding, hiding, and avoiding and evading as well.

A lot of what I have to say is depressing and negative. Nevertheless, I invite you to take courage from what I say and begin the work of learning to tell the truth. When I say what people normally do, please take it as a personal invitation to be *abnormal.* The best way to judge what is normal is simply to look into the faces of people walking down the street or on the subway or driving to work. Keep track of how many look happy. In my most recent count, seven out of ten looked either dead or damned unhappy. This is an invitation to abnormality from someone who has tried both normal lying and abnormal truth telling.

Being Abnormally Honest

It is normal to be unhappy; most people are. It is normal to discover that life doesn't live up to its billing. It is normal to be disappointed but getting along and doing the best you can. It's not normal to be honest. What is normal is to be concerned foremost with having a good cover story. Normal people are concerned with figuring out the right thing to say that puts them in the best light. They want to live up to their own best guess about what the people they are talking to want to hear.

An honest person, in contrast, focuses on saying what is so. Getting back to honesty rescues people from being normal. Sanity is getting back to basic, funky, hometown reality, down from the clouds of good cover stories.

What passes for sanity is an agreed-on form of insanity, which is an attempt to make life work out by legislating ideals and imposing values in our own minds and selling them to other minds. It is normal to be insane. Being sane is abnormal. Abnormal, sane, honest people are less worried and more free than normal people. They are, however, less secure. This feeling of being less secure is something you have to get used to. In the beginning it's a burden. Then it becomes a possibility — a possible choice of a way to live — a choice made on purpose. Then it becomes an opportunity for creation.

Learning to Love Insecurity

The person who learns to tell the truth is the most free, most alive kind of adult human being you'll ever see, but is more insecure than normal. The insecurity comes from having fewer beliefs to rely on for security. Although beliefs don't really provide security, they provide an insulation against the world and one feels afraid but protected. Normally, we continue to anticipate catastrophe to justify the protection of our belief systems and to provide a sense of safety. By predicting and guarding against all negative future outcomes, our minds do the best they can to protect us from the unpleasant uncertainty of freedom.

Making unpleasant uncertainty pleasant is like learning to enjoy being scared on a rollercoaster or to enjoy horror movies. The unpleasant uncertainty takes some time to get used to, but eventually becomes tolerable and even exciting. Just like the fun of scaring yourself on a rollercoaster ride, you learn to like the excitement of mild, ongoing risk-taking. This, of course, can become another racket, another act of bravado or attempt to be eccentric and unusual and shocking just to hide fear. But you can also deliberately accustom yourself to uncertainty as a way of life. That paradoxical state — comfortable uncertainty — is a prerequisite for a creative, fulfilling life. Growing and sharing, rather than stagnation, occur in a context of uncertainty.

The liar in you and me is a mine field of catastrophic expectations and hope and hype. The truth teller in you and me is the one of whom e.e. cummings says: "We are human beings; for whom birth is an extremely welcome mystery, the mystery of growing: the mystery which happens only and whenever we are faithful to ourselves. You and I wear the dangerous looseness of doom and find it becoming. Life for eternal us is now; and now is much too busy being a little more than everything to seem anything, catastrophic included."[3]

We have all had a few breakthroughs to the way of being e.e. cummings describes, but they often scare us so badly we crawl back into our minds to escape. Usually when we have a real breakthrough, when we get saved or see the light or get born again, we don't stay in that new state for long. We retreat.

These short breakthrough events are usually preceded by owning up to the truth and disowning previous pretense. We all love that heightened experience and that sense of breathing free, but we can't stand it for long. So usually after we have a breakthrough and escape the mind jail, we quickly build ourselves another nest of beliefs to keep from going out of control. Sometimes we use for building materials our prating words about freedom. Thus, today's liberating insight becomes tomorrow's jail. The truth is immediate, and changes with the moment. The most real truth is temporary and passing. Usually by the time the real truth gets pointed to with words or a finger, it is gone or changed. This ever-changing truth is the truth of experience. Evaluations of the truth of experience are all bullshit. Some bullshit is useful, but not nearly as useful as most of us think. Evaluations are never the truth, although a person may tell the truth about his evaluations and in fact must do so if he is to own them rather than be jailed by them. We all tend to get lost in the swamp of our evaluative minds trying to make decisions and figure out how to behave and what to do next while constantly considering what we imagine others might imagine about us as a result of any action we anticipate taking. This concern about controlling the opinions of others and keeping control of ourselves kills more people than any form of environmental stress. Even worse, most of those who don't die would scarcely know the difference if they did.

We have a hard time, as minded beings, putting up with the nebulous ever-passing truth, the truth of experience. We go for the hard rail of principle to keep from falling down the bumpy stairs of the real temporary ever-dying truth. Even if the principles we rely on are principles of great despair, we would rather be certain than uncertain. We would rather be sure of a correctly predicted negative outcome than face the realistic uncertainty of an unpredictable future even if it includes the possibility of great joy and success. People buy immeasurable loads of bullshit for the illusion of security. We believe security comes from principles and from controlling other people, but security doesn't exist. The only security we have is in our ability to fly by the seat of our pants. The being within which the mind resides yearns for freedom. The mind resists freedom. Freedom is antithetical to mind. The mind exists for survival. The mind was built to provide security, certainty, prediction, and control. The mind has surpassed its function of physical survival to ensure the survival of the "sea of suggestions" it long ago decided it was. The mind is a bullshit machine.

The main thing that can free a person from his or her own mind is telling the truth. Telling the truth is always interpreted by the mind as a threat to its security. When people think that who they are is their mind, they feel like they are committing suicide when they start telling the truth. It scares the shit out of them and they wish it would hurry up and get over with. And they are committing suicide, in a way. What dies in telling the truth is the false self, the image projection we have presented to the world. All real suicides, where people really died, were the result of a battle between being and mind. In those cases the mind won. ➣

TABOOS AGAINST EXCITEMENT

THE HISTORY OF MODERN PSYCHOLOGY is the history of this century's cultural taboos against excitement. Understanding how we (as a society) arrived at our current psychological understanding is useful for any individual in the process of re-claiming his or her identity as the being in which the light came on. History serves us best if it helps us to debunk our belief in ourselves and our taboos.

Psychoanalytic theory emerged in Europe and America at the turn of the century in response to the social phenomenon of Victorian morality, which was dominant in those parts of the world at the time. According to Sigmund Freud, the primary psychological problems of Western persons in his day were the result of sexual repression; that is, people being taught to deny that they had feelings in their genitals. Consequently, his theory concerned sexuality and its repression and expression. Freud sought to cure, in individual cases, the cultural sickness of guilt about being sexual.

In the years since then we haven't solved our sexual problems, but the intensity with which we have to deny our sexual nature has definitely decreased. Sex is not such a shame any more. There are still, however, all kinds of controls we are supposed to put on our sexual excitement — to pretend that it's not there or to avoid getting too excited. A major social concern is how to be assured of control over *other people's* excitement. We make deals with other people not to let our excitement get out of hand if they will not let theirs get out of hand. We don't want to embarrass each other.

The problem with denying sexual energy is that, sooner or later, somehow or other, it has to be dealt with. Repression doesn't really make things go away. The feelings and excitement that are so bothersome to us resurface in other areas of our lives. For instance, a person who has put a lot of energy into denying his own sexuality and making sexual behavior an evil thing may become a self-appointed defender of the public morals and will make it his civic duty to screen pornographic movies and books in a tireless effort to protect the young people of this country from filth. This may be the only way he can deal with his own sexual feelings without violating what his mind believes is acceptable behavior. Most of us, however, don't go to this extreme. We suppress our sexuality with guilt, moralism, and compensating forms of excitement like overeating, overworking, smoking cigarettes, taking drugs, drinking, and so on. We keep ourselves busy thinking, eating, working hard, and using alternative tranquilizers and stimulants rather than staying in touch with the sensations in our bodies.

After a couple of world wars in which people killed each other in large numbers, it became obvious that society had another serious sickness in addition to sexual repression: the repression of anger. Fritz Perls wrote a book called *Ego, Hunger and Aggression* in the 1940s, in which he developed a theory concerning the causes and treatment of aggression. He said that people had to learn how to make aggressing a *process* of personal psychological growth instead of a *cause.* Just as the person watching pornographic movies as a censor would probably benefit from dealing with his own repressed sexual feelings instead of fighting for the anti-smut cause, people would benefit more from dealing with anger on a personal level than they would from collectively warring on other groups of people.

The warfare going on inside us, disowned, gets projected into the outside world. We make our enemies the very picture of evil, justifying our anger at the same time we avoid the immediate experience of it. Instead of an immediate argument or fight, we think hateful thoughts. Since we are frightened of our anger, we learn to *think* rather than *act* when we get angry. Most people think that this is the way to handle anger. It takes a toll, however, in terms of feeling alive and happy, and creates more anger. In order to decrease the pressure, we have to get mad out loud, but we are afraid of the experience of anger we would have to go through in order to have the anger disappear. We learn to "act nice" and deny that we are angry, and we make ourselves sick in the process of denial. *This is one of the main areas in which something we can't tell the truth about ruins our lives.* The ongoing denial process uses a lot of energy and thought. Thus, the angry feelings we try to control end up controlling us. They keep us fat as we eat to suppress them, or alienated and more alone as we act even nicer to control them.

When we are willing to experience our anger and raise hell

with others, our anger disappears or changes form after a period of heated exchange. When we begin to acknowledge the unacknowledged aggression and repressed anger, it no longer runs our lives. Usually a few other unacknowledged emotions show up too. In fact, there are always other feelings underneath the anger. Grief may show up next. As it turns out, there is usually a fund of unacknowledged joy buried under the unacknowledged anger and grief. The joy is buried so deep, and was repressed so long ago, that most people never even suspect that it exists inside of them. I believe *joy* is the most primitively repressed emotion, and the one closest to the original source experience of unity in the womb and early life. Children have the freedom to express joy openly. Adults repress joy. It is a way of protecting ourselves from being hurt. Just as we fear the consequences of expressing anger or sexual feelings, we fear the consequences of giving and receiving love. God forbid we should get too happy! If we let ourselves bubble over, we fear that we just might bubble away. We are afraid that if we let ourselves love freely, we'll be opening ourselves up for tremendous hurt. Joy and expressions of love are thus the primary repressed emotions and actions. We don't trust happiness. We preserve the superstition that if we get too happy we're in for a downfall. We might fall back into heaven and lose track of ourselves altogether.

Neurosis

Neurosis is essentially a refusal to accept what is happening in the present. Neurosis involves denying the truth about any form of excitement, here and now. A neurotic is a person who incessantly demands that life be other than it is. A person refusing to accept what is being experienced in any given moment is being neurotic at that moment. Being neurotic occasionally doesn't qualify one for diagnosis as a neurotic. A person who steals once is only a person who stole something one time. A person who steals over and over is a thief. To the extent that we all occasionally avoid experience, we all occasionally indulge in neurotic behavior. Whether we earn the label neurotic depends only on the frequency, persistence, and intensity with which we deny feelings, sensations, or any experience whatsoever. A person who refuses to acknowledge experience over and over is a neurotic. Thus, neurosis is a name for consistently denying sexuality, aggression, joy, grief, love, and other feelings. The key to the *cure* for neurosis is not only the identification of the feelings being denied, but the person's *acknowledgment* of those feelings. Usually more than one emotion is being denied. For example, when a troubled adolescent breaks down and cries after expressing anger at his father because some event has blown his tough-independence act, he may express authentic anger, authentic grief, authentic love. The truth about what feelings are there cures neurosis.

We get lost in our minds and lose touch with our experience when we begin to feel something that we are afraid is too much for us to feel, or something we think we are not supposed to feel. We are all afraid of having our excitement run away with us, of losing control. When we try to avoid fully experiencing the dreaded sensation or emotion, we get trapped in the frenetic babbling of our minds. Have you ever noticed that after you have had an uncomfortable encounter with someone in which you didn't fully express how you felt at the time, your mind talks to you incessantly? It keeps reviewing the conversation, trying to insert things you wished you had said. Our minds get energy to babble on like this from our fear of experiencing dreaded emotions, and they work overtime to keep our attention away from what we're afraid to feel. Recapturing control of your own attention is thus the first step to overcoming neurosis.

Refocusing Our Awareness

A human being can only be aware of three things: *1.* things happening in the immediate environment, *2.* feelings and sensations inside the body, and *3.* thoughts and fantasies. Most of us spend most of our time paying attention to the third category, the mind-stream, and have lost touch with what is actually happening inside our skin and right in front of us. We fall into the habit of giving all of our attention to thoughts, beliefs, and fantasy, and thus we lose touch with the basis of all fantasy: experience. Good therapy helps people who are trapped in the mindstream, or in their thoughts about experience. It helps them get back to paying attention to what's going on here and now.

Refocusing on experience helps the person in denial to feel what is going on inside him and begin to tell the truth to cure himself. He may learn that the source of his bodily sensations are his beliefs and fears based on earlier incomplete and unpleasant experiences where he made a moral resolve never to let anything like that happen again. People stay scared and thought-ridden until they get some support from other people who have been through the experience of lightening up and letting go of protective beliefs and taboos. Once a person comes to his senses, he can learn to rely less and less on his mind's ideas and beliefs, and really *know* from moment to moment how he feels. Again, as Fritz Perls put it, the objective is to "lose your mind and come to your senses." When a therapist can help a person to tolerate living in a wider experience of life in any given moment, the way that person relates to his whole life is transformed. The transformation from living in the narrow jail of belief to living in the wide world of experience is at first terrifying, but, as those who have hung in there can tell you, it's well worth the trouble.

Applied Psychology

What follows are conversations recalled from a few sessions with a client. The interaction demonstrates the way refocusing on experience rather than the conversations of the mind is both frightening and intensely worthwhile.

Stephanie started therapy because she wanted to lose weight. She was 23, had a receptionist job she disliked, and wanted to lose 30 pounds. She was shy and mildly depressed, and particularly unhappy about being fat. She was also very pretty and, overweight or not, had a voluptuous figure. In fact, I imagined her being overweight had a lot to do with her attractiveness. During our first conversation I said, "I think you're pretty, and overweight or not, your figure is still very sexy." She blushed and said, "Thank you." I said, "I imagine that men 'hit on you' and come on to you all the time." She nodded and smiled. Then the following dialogue ensued:

Me: "How do you feel about that?"

Stephanie: "Well, at first I'm flattered, I guess, but really I don't like it too much. When the men at the office make little wisecracks, I don't say anything, but I don't like it."

There was silence for a while.

Me: "I imagine when you start to lose weight, your figure is going to be even more noticeable than it is now. You're going to have more of that to deal with. You'll have to create some other way of handling men hitting on you besides getting fat again."

Stephanie: "Yes, I know what you're talking about. I don't know what I'm going to do, but I've quit diets before for that very reason."

Me: "Well, what about right now? I'm attracted to you. And I'm telling you — are you embarrassed?"

Stephanie: "Yes, a little. Although it isn't as bad as at work."

Me: "Are you attracted to me?"

"A little bit," she said and looked down and blushed.

"I notice that you're looking down and turning red." We both laughed. "Sure is a shame we're attracted to each other, isn't it?" We laughed again.

She said, "I don't really think it's shameful, but I do feel embarrassed. I talk to my girlfriend Shelly about this all the time. I think it's funny, and I also feel kind of sad in a way. I don't know why."

"I appreciate you for being willing to talk to me about this. I want to talk to you about attraction and embarrassment and sadness. I also want you to know that we can talk about these things without having to make a pass at each other. I'm married. I won't come on to you, and you don't have to worry about that with me. But I like your smile, and I like your willingness to talk with me about this. I'm happy when you say you're attracted to me." We both laughed again.

"I like this, too. I never would have brought this up with anyone else, but I'm glad that we're talking about it. Usually, I would wait and tell Shelly later that I thought you were cute and liked me. Actually, I'm kind of relieved that you're married." We laughed again. Laughter is the sound of freedom. We liked each other.

"I noticed something else about you."

"Go ahead; this is interesting," Stephanie prompted me.

"I notice that you are very quick to smile even when you talk about being angry or you're embarrassed. I imagine everybody thinks of you as a 'nice girl.'"

Stephanie laughed. "Yeah, I guess so. All the women at the office call me "dear." They think I'm sweet."

"Aren't you?"

"No; it's an act."

We both laughed again. She continued.

"Shelly and I talk about this, too. I think I have to be nice all the time, or that it isn't right to get angry. I get mad, but I don't show it."

"A lot of people eat when that happens."

"Oh, I do that all the time — and so does everyone else in my office." We both laughed again.

"Later, when you start eating less and working out more, you might feel more anger. You won't be handling your anger by eating like you used to. You will get a chance to experience the feelings you've been dampening down with food. Sometimes it's not much fun. You'll either have to figure out some other way of dealing with those feelings or you won't be successful with weight loss or depression for long."

She paused. "Okay...It sounds like more trouble than I thought."

"It probably is. But it's not all bad news. You'll probably feel okay most of the time. We will make some agreements about exercise and diet. I will teach you self-hypnosis and ask you to practice it on your own. We will do some work with you telling me about who you get mad at and when. I'll be asking you to do things like go have a conversation with people you have been hiding things from, like your parents or friends. There will be times when you may feel like quitting. You may hit a plateau, where you won't lose any weight for a while even though you're being 'good.' You may get depressed, angry or tired. You may not feel any of those things. If you are willing to let those feelings come up and experiment with them, without quitting, you have a chance of staying thin for a year which will give you good odds for staying relatively thin permanently. I am not sure you should do this though. Being mildly depressed and overweight has worked pretty well for you. I'm not sure you ought to give it up."

"Ha!...I do know what you mean, though. But I'm tired of all of it. I'm ready to figure out another way."

Later on, we talked a little more. She told me how it was a hassle for her to be living at home, and that while work was okay, she sometimes got headaches there and generally felt tired after she got home. She also volunteered that she had been uncomfortable about her figure for some time. She said she developed very early in adolescence and remembered feeling embarrassed when men would pay attention to her while she was with her father. Her father felt uncomfortable about her voluptuous figure as well and would say, "Stephanie, wear clothes that aren't so revealing!" She had been hiding her body under bulky sweaters and blazers since she was ten years old.

I believe her willingness to share these personal feelings with me grew out of the context created by my willingness to tell her what I was feeling and thinking about her, and my asking her to do the same.

Anger, Sex and Diet

What Stephanie now needs to do in order to lose 30 pounds and keep it off is to stop being ashamed of being sexually attractive and to acknowledge her attractiveness openly. She needs to stop faking pleasantness and sweetness when she feels angry and she needs to tell people where to get off. This may take some time for her to learn, and a therapist can assist her by creating the context in which that learning may occur, by sharing his own experience, and by encouraging her to give 'em hell when she feels like it.

That couple of sessions with Stephanie was done in a context of permission, granted by an authority, where it was okay to talk about feelings she thought she shouldn't talk about, while she was having them. That let her give herself permission to experience and acknowledge out loud to a man some of the taboo and uncomfortable feelings she had been avoiding. As therapist, my willingness to talk about the immediate issue of our attraction to each other, and the honest way we talked, created a context for dealing with the issues of sex and anger out loud. A taboo was violated: her secret thoughts came out and were expressed in front of a male in a context of no danger. Eventually she would be coached to come out of the closet with the truth about her feelings in situations with men whom she used to consider dangerous, and she could discover that she need not be as careful as she thought.

A context is like a big bowl into which everything about a personality is included and considered acceptable. The context that a person on a diet creates has to include occasional binges, wanting to quit entirely, feeling excited and energetic, getting a headache, feeling scared, and irritable, and turned on, and angry, and happy, and depressed, and confused. It also may include occasional plateaus, looking at what she really wants to do with her life, and being afraid to change. The more help a therapist gives a client to create that context for herself, the more successfully the client will handle what comes up when the therapist is not around. The therapist does this by sharing his or her experience and by giving the client an idea of what the work is all about. The purpose is not to scare or warn the client, but rather to encourage her right from the start to be willing to experience whatever comes up as part of being a creator of her life rather than a victim of previously learned ways of handling life. These previously learned methods of adaptation to life *do* work. Getting drunk works. Getting stoned works. Being overweight works. Being sad works, particularly in a world where being angry or horny or expressively joyful are taboo. These are all methods of survival, and if they get replaced there is a risk that the new replacement will be a big pain to accomplish and not work as well as the old way. Problems that seem unacceptable start looking better after a little suffering that is greater than that associated with the problem. This is why the context for each person's commitment to change has to include a perspective that allows for periods of greater discomfort than that caused by the problem they are trying to fix.

Stephanie has suppressed a lot of resentment towards men about the wisecracks they make about her body. Perhaps she will find a way to express that resentment effectively. Perhaps not. It is important to realize, however, that anger is not the only excitement she eats to avoid. She must come up with a way to handle the excitement of having men pay attention to her. She handled that excitement before by tranquilizing it with food in the short run, and by getting fatter. By becoming less exciting to others, she eventually resolved the anxiety of being uncomfortably excited herself. If she loses a certain amount of weight she'll get down to where she is exciting and excited again. She'll have to deal with that excitement another way or gain the weight back. She may have to admit that the excitement she was avoiding was her own. It is partly her own response to the men's attention that scares her or makes her feel uncomfortable. Getting fat allows people who are uncomfortable about their own sexual excitement to be emotionally intimate with members of the opposite sex while remaining physically isolated from them. In this way, they remain safe from their own sexuality.

Saying "no" is not a problem when we mean "no." It's saying "no" to wanting to say "yes" from which Stephanie has protected herself by gaining weight. Her weight greatly diminished her opportunities to say "no" or "yes." She will have to confront this choice, and make it each time it comes up, rather than avoid the experience of lust.

We can salute the genius of minds that come up with neurotic solutions to problems. People do the best they can, and they do a pretty good job of surviving and handling a lot of conflicting interests. I congratulate the mind that comes up with each creative, ingenious solution — and I respect it.

I think effectiveness in maintaining weight-loss is one of the most graphic ways of determining the effectiveness of psychotherapy. When I support someone in losing weight and keeping it off, I must respectfully request his mind to *come up with another answer.* People who lose weight successfully come up with other answers. People who don't lose weight successfully fail to come up with other answers. Across the board, on all diets, only about 12% of the people who lose weight maintain the loss for a year. Statistics about weight-loss are probably very much reflective of the likelihood of any lasting psychological change. People who are able to make a certain diet work can probably make any diet work. The other 88% want to lose weight, and do for a while, but can't sustain the change. I think that about 12% of the people who go for any psychological change make it stick. The help of a good therapist makes these statistics a little better. Not many people sustain real change without support in creating a context called "going through what has been previously avoided or kept secret." Some people do it on their own with friends who aren't therapists. No one really does it alone.

Each innocent new life comes out of that eternity of blissful timelessness in the womb and begins to learn to control, distinguish, name, and manipulate the parts of the world that get distinguished. There are as many ways to be embroiled in that process as there have been human beings in history. Behind these millions and millions of ways of being, human beings have always shared a unitary hum, a sense of being, and a common history of having lived in eternal bliss in the womb. What has also always been there is the possibility of identifying with that beingness rather than identifying exclusively with the unique adaptation the being came up with to survive in the world.

As we grow up, we descend from heaven and ascend into hell. We come down from the heaven of the womb and we grow up into the hell of civilized, acculturated neurosis. Salvation is the rediscovery of ourselves as being. To escape the hard-earned, hard-built prison of the self, we must reinterpret our identities to include more than that prison. We must re-identify ourselves to include the more primitive and universally-shared self that we all were and are and evermore shall be. When this power gets tapped, it can be used for such mundane things as losing weight or making a living as well as for a complete turnaround in life. To recognize and accept the mind's way of adapting to the world for the sake of survival is the first step on the way back home to the hum. Resistance to one's case-history self, particularly *trying* to change that self, keeps one trapped in one's case history. Acceptance of one's case-history self allows one to get over it. When psychotherapy works, the person loosens her identification with her own case history and identifies with her being, the one who has been there since the light came on in the womb, the one who is electrical and alive and able to pay attention, second by second, heartbeat by heartbeat, present-moment by present-moment. ⌒

HOW TO DEAL WITH ANGER

"We human beings are Homo Hostilus,
*the hostile species, the enemy-making animal.
We are driven to fabricate an enemy as a scapegoat
to bear the burden of our denied enmity."*
— Sam Keen

A FAMOUS WAR STORY tells of a platoon of soldiers who had been fighting together as a unit for some time. One night, an enemy soldier lobbed a grenade into their midst. For a few seconds everyone froze. Suddenly, a private dove on the grenade with his helmet. It detonated under him. The man was destroyed, but the other men were saved by his heroism.

One outstanding characteristic of human beings is that they are sometimes willing to sacrifice their lives to save others. Such acts of courage are honored, as they should be, as the highest expression of love.

Many of us deal with anger in much the same way as the private in the story deals with the grenade. We consider anger a life-threatening experience. Anger wells up in us, seemingly from out of nowhere, and we imagine it will injure everyone we love if we let it go off. Without even thinking, we smother the anger the way the private smothered the grenade. We sacrifice ourselves to protect our friends and family.

What makes meaningless sacrifices look like heroism is ignorance. History is full of pitiful, wonderful, dumb-assed heroes who sacrificed their lives to save those they loved from some bullshit threat that seemed real at the time but turned out to be imaginary. The tragedy of the useless sacrifice of life has been around for as long as human beings have been around and will remain central to the definition of humanity until we learn to create ourselves differently.

Our greatest heroism, our willingness to surrender life itself for our loved ones, and our greatest tragedy, the mistaken and useless sacrifice of our own and others' lives for meaningless causes, are central to the tragic joke we are.

Nowhere is the waste of courage and love better demonstrated than in everyday cases of the unsung heroes of anger. In every case, the hero is a fool. His courage is wasted. The hero's fear of the devastating effect of anger is entirely unrealistic. He or she overestimates the destructive power of anger and feels that it must be controlled even if it means sacrificing his or her life. What is even worse is that the poor fool dies over and over again, a little piece at a time. Anger is not a grenade.

Many of us consider ourselves to be heroes and heroines when we are just damned fools. Only the people who live with such heroic fools seem to recognize them for what they are. Such recognition exacerbates the problem, for nothing pisses your average fool off more than having to live with a damned ingrate who doesn't appreciate the heroic sacrifices that have been made for his or her benefit. To make things worse, the "damned ingrate" usually sees himself or herself as another unappreciated hero, sacrificing self-expression for the health of the relationship.

As we accumulate resentment for not being appreciated for sacrificing our lives to protect others, our acts of love and courage become poisoned memories. The person who loved you and whom you used to love becomes the biggest pain-in-the-ass of your life.

The contrast between self-perception and perception by others stands out clearly in my work with couples and families, in which I am privy to the ongoing arguments between martyr-heroes and hero-martyrs. People really get mad when they're *resented* for withholding anger — something for which they feel they *should be appreciated.* But, contrary to popular belief, people resent being withheld from and lied to. Withheld anger destroys relationships by sucking the aliveness out of them. For aliveness to be restored, both to the relationships and the individual, anger must be expressed.

Direct and Indirect Expressions of Anger

How does a person used to suppressing anger learn to express anger? It takes practice. The *way* anger is expressed has everything to do with the outcome of an argument. When anger is expressed in such a way that both people are fully present to the experience, the anger eventually goes away, and the people have a new opening in their relationship.

Anger is universal, but methods of expression vary. The continuum of expression ranges from murder to total suppression and cover-up. The continuum can be divided into two parts, indirect expression and direct expression. All indirect forms are sick and stupid. Many direct forms fail as well. Many people have tried to express anger directly at one time or another but given up because, as some have said, "it only seemed to make things worse." It does make things worse for a short time, but much better over the long run. When people don't get good results from the direct expression of anger, the odds are the anger wasn't completely expressed. Probably one or both people were mad, but trying to be decent and fair at the same time. Trying to be constructive while wanting to destroy is a real dilemma, a division of energy between opposing goals, and confusing. Divided expression doesn't work. *This self-opposition with regard to expressing anger is what perpetuates anger.* To express anger fully, we must give up most of our constraints on it. We can inhibit killing and physical violence. But we must be willing to be angry *rather than* decent and fair, because angry, rather than decent and fair, is what we presently are. After we are angry, we may be decent and fair, but we will never be authentically angry *or* authentically fair while we are struggling to be both at once.

Anger is Universally Human, Ways of Handling Anger Are Culturally Varied

It is human to feel angry, just as it is human to feel love, desire, or fear. Anger is not in itself a problem. Children periodically get mad, raise hell, and get over it. Sometimes they win and get their way and sometimes they lose, but they usually get over it. Adults, however, persist in using *learned ways of handling anger that don't work*. This attachment to fruitless strategies — not the anger itself — is the problem.

Anger is bound to happen to all human beings from being little, less strong, and dependent on others for a long, long time. It seems like it takes forever to get big. All children get mad in all cultures. Some babies are fussier than others to start with, but all babies are in for disappointment as they grow older. The older they grow, the more disappointments they experience. And they protest angrily. Parental response to these early instances of protest are the start of long-term cultural conditioning.

As soon as we become capable of having expectations we become capable of protesting not having them met. As Norman O. Brown points out in *Life Against Death*,[1] if being neurotic is protesting against the world being as it is, neurosis is built in to growing up. As I said in the previous chapter, *being* a neurotic is *incessantly* demanding, in a rigid stylized form, that the world be other than it is. If someone gets drunk a few times she hasn't yet qualified as an alcoholic, but if she persists she earns the right to the category. On numerous occasions, and at all stages of growing up, all of us behave neurotically. Whether we adopt the neurotic protest as a stand in life, as an incessant theme, and as a way of being depends on a lot of factors, the most important of which is how we handle the anger that comes with disappointed expectations.

In our culture, when we are older we still experience anger, but we no longer permit ourselves to *be* angry and to express anger at the same time. Therefore we don't get over it as quickly as we did when we were younger. We learn, in the course of growing up, after getting punished for anger and losing a few battles, that it is smarter to hide our anger than to express it. We are raised to believe that we should get angry only at certain times, at certain people, and only if we are "right." Since we all get angry all the time, at the wrong people, at the wrong times, and for the wrong reasons, we learn early in life that the way to deal with this unwanted anger is to keep it hidden.

We cannot avoid unwanted experiences at the wrong times toward the wrong people — like sexual excitement and anger — just by thinking we shouldn't be having them. Denial, the most primitive and least effective defense against these feelings, stubbornly persists even though it never works. When we deny anger, the way we perceive the world and the way we conceive of the people in it become distorted. The rest of our lives are colored by the distorted perception of the world resulting from the stockpile of denied and withheld anger.

The little nests of morality tales about anger that make up our Judeo-Christian-Greek culture, that our children learn from fairy tales and schooling, don't help them to handle anger.

Displacement

When anger is not expressed directly, it is expressed indirectly. So it gets expressed but not experienced. If anger is not *expressed* directly, it is not *experienced* directly. Unless a person experiences anger in the body and acknowledges the experience, the anger does not complete itself — does not discharge, subside, and go away. When anger is expressed indirectly, in ways that are calculated to avoid the experience of anger, anger gets stored up rather than dissipating. The experience of anger is converted to thoughts about the resented person — judgments, complaints, conclusions, and imaginary conversations. When you are preoccupied with thoughts about someone toward whom you are angry, you become distracted. "You're driving me to distraction!" my mother used to say. Forgetting agreements, standing people up, mildly criticizing most of another's behavior, having accidents, making mistakes, accidentally saying things to hurt others, and forgetting people's names are all indirect expressions of anger.

Anger of this kind *is* dangerous, much more so than the short-term explosive kind. This is the form of anger with which we have been poisoned and with which we continue to poison our children. This form of anger accumulates and is the direct cause of the frequency of physical abuse in our society.

As difficult as it may be for our minds to accept, the direct expression of resentment works *better* than the suppression of anger to protect ourselves and each other from damage by anger. When we communicate our resentment to the person we resent, the anger dissipates more completely in the moment of expression. The anger may get cranked up to a higher pitch than seems reasonable in many small arguments, but the intensity of the experience allows the heat out where it can cool. People can get over being mad if they face resentment one instance at a time. Even if the person toward whom we are angry doesn't change, agree to change, or apologize, we can still forgive that person for our own benefit.

The extreme alternative to this one-step-at-a-time approach is to be the youngest kid to make Eagle Scout in Boy Scout history, get good grades, always be nice, become a good Marine and then go up in the tower at the University of Texas and shoot to kill everybody in sight for two hours.

Displaced anger is the problem of the age. The people who died on battlefields in the 20th century all died in the defense of some principle of rightness. Most of them were just kids. Most of them were being obedient and righteous. Most of them were scared. Most were pissed off, they thought, at some common enemy of the time in the socially approved way. Most of them were fighting to save their loved ones from some ignorant fucking thing or another. Most of them were adolescents ganging together in a common cause of righteous murder to protect their God-damned parents who taught them to handle their anger that way. These kids, who were polite to their mothers and obedient to their fathers, were pitiful ignorant heroes, and the sacrifice of their lives was a waste.

So this is what happens with anger: as children grow, constantly overpowered, cared for, and controlled, childhood expressions of anger against stronger adults are punished, either overtly or covertly, or worse, condescendingly moralized about. As children, we do the best we can to copy approved ways of dealing with anger to avoid getting punished for it. The result, at least in our culture, is that most people don't express anger directly. It's not that they don't know they're angry or that they won't talk about their anger; they do and they will. Most people, however, won't express their resentment in person to the person at whom they are angry. Instead, they gossip, complain, criticize, fantasize about telling the person off, and let it out in other indirect ways.

Suppression and displacement to ideals, indignation, and judgments (against others and ourselves) usually work well enough that by the time we males reach 18 years of age and some elder asshole tells us to kill some people to defend some bullshit principle, we run right out and do it.

Undoing the Learned Suppression of Anger
Overcoming completely the learned suppression of anger is, I think, a futile objective. Some people do become less angry, and less crippled by denial, through therapy. Some people come to terms with their anger and acknowledge its influence on their lives to a greater degree and become less helpless when angry. Others don't have much luck with it. Everyone who experiments with telling the truth about anger at least finds out that people don't die if you tell them you resent them for something they said or did. In fact, more often than not, when people tell the truth about their feelings, relationships get better, even if the truth is about hatred.

The transition from being a foolish hero or heroine to being free of the fear of anger is a therapeutic process you can engage in by agreement with people with whom you have committed relationships. Expressing resentment directly is a requirement for creating an authentic relationship between two human beings instead of an entanglement of two minds. Agreeing to tell the truth about anger in a committed relationship is a way to get over some of the damage and suffering that comes from how you were raised. It is a way of losing your mind and coming to your senses and experiencing yourself as a being, rather than as a jumble of morals gleaned from whatever your sad story may be. It is a way of growing beyond primitive foolishness to a more advanced form.

Telling the Truth About Anger for the Sake of Forgiveness
Telling the truth about anger means making a present-tense statement about your experience, *while angry*, to the person with whom you are angry. No one can have much luck getting over anger-sickness unless they can tell the truth about their experience in the present and in the presence of the person they are mad at. I'm not saying you *should* tell the truth in order to be a good or better person. This is not meant as a moral principle, but as a functional rule of thumb. Telling the truth about your anger lets you function better in a pragmatic way, achieving your goals and enjoying the process, instead of feeling driven by forces beyond your control. When you are willing to have an experience *be as it is*, prior to categorizing the experience as "good" or "bad," and you don't waste all of your energy trying to avoid or lie about the experience, you have a choice about how you can respond to that experience.

One of the hallmarks of suppressed anger is helplessness. The language of helplessness is "I can't;" "they made me;" "it's no use;" "it doesn't really matter;" and "you just don't understand." Power is assigned to forces outside the speaker.

The following example of a couple's interaction in my office illustrates an angry client being directed to make a present-tense statement about her experience, rather than remaining lost in her mind.

Therapist: "Anne, I want you to look at David and tell him what you resent him for."

Anne (looks at David and then back at the therapist): "He never listens to me. I can't talk to him about anything important and he has no interest in my life."

Therapist: "Look at David and tell him, not me."

Anne (looks at David and reddens): "You never listen to me. I can't talk to you." She looks back at the therapist for approval.

David: "Oh, bullshit. I listen to you."

Anne glances at her husband, then makes a "See what I mean?" gesture to the therapist.

Therapist: "Anne, first of all, I want you to keep looking at David, not at me, and allow yourself to remain in touch with him even if you start to feel uncomfortably angry. Secondly, be more specific. Complete the sentence 'I resent you for....' with something he actually said or did."

Anne: "I'm *not* angry; I'm just upset about not being listened to. He treats me like a child and I'm sick of putting up with it."

Therapist: "You're lying. You *are* angry, and you're unwilling so far to experiment with your anger to see what would happen if you were direct instead of indirect and poisonous in your expression of it. If you could tell him directly and expressively what you resent him for, you may find that you feel less helpless and less dominated by David. "

Anne: "I knew you'd take his side! You're just like a prosecuting attorney putting a rape victim on trial. I don't need to spend two hours and all this money to be berated; I can stay home and get that for free."

(David has been reacting throughout this exchange with dramatic sighs, scowls, and derisive laughter. Anne now turns to face him.)

Anne: "I resent you for laughing at me, you...you...shithead!" (Tears have welled up in her eyes.)

Therapist: "Good! Keep going!"

Anne (holding out her hand for a tissue): "I can't...it makes me cry and I don't want to cry." (She attempts to retain control of her tears; she closes her eyes, blows her nose, and then covers her face with her hands. After a moment, she lifts her head and faces David again.) "I resent you for laughing at me just now; I resent you for laughing at me whenever I'm serious. I resent you for...for...for never listening to me."

They stare at each other. Anne has stopped crying. Her face is red and blotchy; her body is rigid; her breathing is rapid. David looks serious now, and his jaw muscles work. He is just perceptibly nodding.

Therapist: "Good, Anne. How do you feel right now?"

Anne (takes a deep breath): "Okay."

Therapist: "'Okay' is an evaluation. I want a *description* of what you are feeling in your body."

Anne: "I'm tense all over. My...my...I'm breathing fast. My hands are shaking."

David: "Your face is red."

Anne: "*Fuck* you!"

David: "Fuck *you!*"

They look at each other.

Therapist: "Good. David, you'll get your turn to express all your resentment, but I want to focus on Anne and have her complete hers first. Anne, keep going, you're doing great. Staying in touch with your experience *in your body*, tell David *specifically* what you resent him for."

Anne: "I resent you for telling me my face was red. I resent you for NOT LISTENING TO ME, YOU ARROGANT SONOF-ABITCH!" (She throws her tissue at him.)

Therapist: "Good! *What specific things has he said or done that you interpreted as him not listening to you?*"

Anne (pauses, considers): "He turns on the TV when I'm in the middle of saying something to him. I can be saying that Martians are invading and the kitchen is on fire, and he'll go, 'Wait a sec, it's third down.'"

Therapist: "When did he last do this?"

Anne: "Um...Monday, I came home from work and I was telling him how upset I was about not getting this project that he *knew* was so important to me and he totally ignored me!"

David: "Jesus, Anne, you started talking to me right in the middle of a game and it was an important part and I just asked you to wait until the commercial to tell me!"

Anne (to Therapist): "Do you think it's too much to ask to stop watching a football game for a few minutes to pay attention to your obviously distraught wife?"

David: "You purposely bring up these melodramas when I'm in the middle of something!"

Anne: "*Melo*dramas!"

Therapist: "Wait, wait.... You're both getting sidetracked into trying to prove, and get me to adjudicate, the rightness of your cases. Instead of focusing on the legality of your positions, I want you to focus on your anger and your experience and *express your anger without having to justify it.* Anne, tell David you resent him for what he did Monday night and make it good and loud and direct and *without justification.*"

Anne (takes a deep breath, turns back to David): "I resent you for turning to the football game as I was talking to you about my project!"

Therapist: "What do you notice in your experience?"

Anne: "I'm feeling sort of...charged up. Tingling."

Therapist: "Say the same resentment again, with more expression."

Anne: "*I resent you for watching the football game while I was talking to you about not getting my project!*" She stops, looking at David, breathing more quickly. She leans forward. "I RESENT YOU FOR WATCHING THE GODDAMN FOOTBALL GAME WHILE I WAS TRYING TO TELL YOU SOMETHING!!!" she shouts, rising out of her chair. She is shaking; her hair is flying; her fists are clenched. She sits back down, panting.

Therapist: "What do you notice?"

Anne: "I feel a lot of energy. I'm certainly not crying anymore." She laughs.

David: "What's so funny?"

Anne: "I don't know. Partly it feels good just to let loose. Partly, I'm laughing because I just realized that my mother used to complain to my dad all the time for the same thing. It's like it's the same goddamned football game from thirty years ago, still on." She laughs again.

The point of this work is clear. With patience and repetition, the client learns to be mad and pay attention to experience in her body at the same time. Anne eventually got in touch with her experience of resentment, and after a while got over it. What came out after she wasn't so mad at David anymore was her resentment for her father for ignoring her, for giving her advice, for being cold when she made less than perfect grades, for criticizing her boyfriends, and so on. The anger that she was denying by claiming helplessness resulted in her saying she "couldn't" talk to her husband. It had a history in her belief about "not being able" to talk to her father. Later, she had a dialogue with an empty chair in which she imagined her father sitting. She switched sides back and forth, becoming at one time her father and another time herself. In this imaginary situation she told her father all the things she resented him for quite expressively and then played *him* telling *her* his resentments.

Later on in therapy, she agreed to spend three days with her father, and tell him her resentments, and stay in touch with her experience. She ended up going on vacation with David and both her parents. When she came back from that trip, she was elated. This is what she said: "When I left there, I was willing and even excited by the prospect of seeing my father again. For the first time I can remember, I thought something other than, 'well, I got through that visit.' While we were still at the beach with my parents, David and I talked about our relationship and about my relationship with my father. We argued some, and we both cried some. We came up with some new ground rules for our marriage — including telling the truth to each other. One night, he and my dad and mom and I stayed up until 2:30 in the morning talking about everything, including what pisses us off about each other, but also about what we appreciate and a bunch of other stuff. We had a great time!"

Admitting Being Upset, Denying Being Angry

Generally, people are willing to admit that they feel "upset," but not that they are angry. We remember, "If you can't say anything nice about someone, don't say anything at all." Forget that. Do the reverse. And when expressing anger, it works better to over-state the case. Since we too often underplay anger, it is necessary to overplay it.

Most of us don't know how to identify clearly what anger feels like inside our bodies. We attend to our many racing thoughts, focusing on the rightness or wrongness of the conversation we just had instead of tuning in to our experience in the moment. We ignore our racing heart and the flush of heat in our face and the tension building in our shoulders and the tightening of our stomachs. When we do acknowledge these feelings, we do so only at an abstract level that subsumes too much experience. We say we are "upset" about some general set of behaviors on someone else's part. Even acknowledging "upset" is a first step; some of us deny even that. The second step is admitting that our "upset" is anger. The third step is speaking resentments specifically and in contact with one's own body and the eyes of the other person.

Other Clues about Denial of Anger

Lots of behaviors indicate anger. If you gossip about someone to someone else, you are angry. You haven't completely expressed your resentment to that person you gossiped about. Another tipoff is breaking your word while *trying* not to. When you find yourself "trying," struggling, striving without any results, look for whom you are trying to please: you are probably mad at them.

Another clue is self-condemnation. Instead of condemning yourself and calling yourself a rotten, weak, or stupid person, ask yourself, "Who am I mad at?" Don't let yourself off the hook with the rationalization, "I'm just mad at myself." This is worthless. You postulate two people, "I" and "myself" who are mad at each other. Put the two pieces back together and find someone else to be mad at. When you have a choice of being mad at someone else or mad at yourself, always pick someone else. Most people think self-condemnation is a virtue; it's not.

Another hint of hidden anger is perfectionism. People who are proud of being perfectionists and for whom hardly anything is ever good enough are angry at someone else.

"Love your neighbor as yourself" doesn't mean to lie; it means to tell the petty, unreasonable, unjustifiable truth — good and loud and direct. Try treating other people as shitty as you treat yourself. At times, being honest about your anger is the only way you have of sharing who you are. Love is sharing what you have, even if you're having a fit. Telling the truth *is* loving your neighbor.

Stupid Questions, Dumb Ideas and Bullshit Rationalizations
People ask me, "Why do I have to express my anger directly to another person? Isn't it possible to just forget about it or just

understand the other person's situation and forgive him?" The answer is no. You cannot forgive someone else without express-ing your resentment directly to her or him. We can all make up plenty of legitimate-sounding reasons for continuing to avoid or withhold from the resented person. "There's no point in bring-ing it up again. It's over. And, besides, I'm not angry anymore" (Then why do you keep thinking about it? Why do you keep bringing it up?). "I believe in forgiveness" (as if "believing" in forgiveness could make you forgive somebody when you haven't). "She probably didn't mean what she said. She just had a really bad day" (as if you could reason yourself out of the experience of being angry). "I can't even remember what I was mad about" (meaning, "I'd rather not remember so I don't have to feel un-comfortable"). "I think I do the same things that I accuse him of doing, so I can't really blame him" (but you do blame him). "She has many other wonderful qualities. I don't want to harp on the negatives" (so you lose touch with your appreciation of her soon after you lose touch with your resentment).

All these explanations sound forgiving and noble, which they would be if they were experiences rather than ideas. The problem is not that these ideas are inaccurate or wrong. The problem is that *ideas* about forgiveness are not forgiveness. They don't even help. What you are left with is the experience of resentment and the concept of forgiveness — and a deteriorating relationship. These explanations are generated by your mind so that you can avoid the experience of anger. As you are saying or thinking these thoughts, you are busying yourself to avoid feeling anger.

Forgiving someone with whom you are angry — actually

experiencing forgiving him — only happens after you tell him what he did or said that you resent. Only when you allow yourself to experience and express anger openly will it disappear.

Thinking and deciding what to do about the person only serves to suppress the anger. Even though you think the anger is over, it will manifest itself in other ways. Your communication will be less honest and spontaneous; you may be more critical of him; you may find being with him more physically tiring, forget appointments with him, and find yourself inexplicably angry at him more and more. After a while, your friendship may feel more superficial than before and you may not like spending as much time with him as you used to. If you live with the person, you may feel a difference in the quality of time you spend together. You may notice that you'd rather stare at the television than look into his eyes.

It takes a lot of courage to change this. You must be willing for things to get worse before they get better.

My Anger May Not Be Right
Most resentments are irrational, unreasonable, stupid, and based on incomplete information. Making a successful case for how your resentment is "right" and how the other person is "wrong" isn't the solution; it's the problem. We human beings are all selfish and unfair and it's worse than useless to pretend we aren't. It is common for children to resent a younger sibling for being the baby of the family. Is that the baby's fault? Did the baby choose to be born last in the family?

It seems unfair to resent people for things over which they

have no control. We're all unfair. It's unreasonable to resent younger siblings, whom we also love, for getting more attention than we do, but the truth is that we still resent them. It's unreasonable to resent parents for growing old, babies for crying, men for being men or women for being women. But we do. Our decision not to express our resentment is based on a deeply held belief that our anger has to be justified, righteous, and legitimate. It doesn't. To be free of anger, we have to give up this belief and allow our resentments and other people's resentments to be expressed even if they are completely irrational.

One of the things that makes getting over the loss of a loved one take a long time is the refusal of people to admit that they are furious at the dead person for dying. It doesn't make sense to hate someone for dying — they didn't do it on purpose. We do, though. Every one of us hates people we love who die on us.

We are psychological beings and not logical beings. So, when you tell the truth about your resentments, you may look like a fool. You will be in good company. The biggest fools of all are the ones wasting their lives pretending not to be fools.

Fairness versus Forgiveness

Many of us are concerned about fairness and use the principle of fairness as our primary rationalization for withholding anger. Advanced instruction in this principle is one reason that many lawyers are fucked-up people and divorces handled with lawyers often end up with children shot back and forth between hostile camps. If you force yourself to be fair, and stay pissed off, you are a fool, and any agreements you make in such a state won't work for you. Judges and lawyers ignore this fact. Judges and lawyers exist for people who can't handle their anger. A judge has to tell you what to do, based on what he or she thinks is fair, whether you like it or not, because you haven't been able to work things out on your own.

There is a better way to fight, that turns out to be equitable, even though it may look uncivilized and unfair in the beginning. It might not seem fair to express what seems like intense resentment for petty reasons in the beginning, but the advantages become clear by the time the argument is over. Things turn out fairly when people get over being angry. The results of experimenting with this kind of interaction are very dramatic.

The major benefit of expressing your anger completely to someone is that afterwards, you can forgive him or her. The reason for forgiving your enemies is not for *their* benefit but for *your own benefit.* Holding grudges against other people doesn't hurt them; doesn't even bother them much — in fact, even pleases them if they are still mad at you. It is not in your enlightened self-interest to hold grudges, regardless of whether it bothers the person you hate or not. Unless you develop the capacity to do what it takes to forgive other people, you can't tell bullshit from reality; you can't forgive yourself; and you stay trapped in moral condemnation in your mind. Your body stays tied in knots and susceptible to illness and you can be sure of a shitty life and lousy relationships with anyone else you pair up with, even if you leave the person you hate.

The "Dangerous Practical Consequences" Rationalization

You might protest, "The reasons I have for not expressing anger deal with real consequences that might ensue if I blew up at someone...for instance, I might lose my job." Yes, you might. However, there is a greater possibility that by not expressing your anger, you will sabotage your relationship with your boss or co-workers to the point where you may as well quit, or will end up quitting or getting fired. Perhaps you start missing days, making mistakes, or just being more interested in making the boss or co-workers wrong than in supporting them, him, or her. Maybe you withhold your enthusiasm a little. The job will become less satisfying, and the rewards of keeping your job will be far outweighed by the aggravation of having to put up with these people. This will occur in direct relation to how much you feel you have to withhold your anger when you are at work. In addition to less satisfaction and poorer performance, the hidden costs include reduced physical health and repercussions in your family life. This isn't to encourage you to lose your job, and it isn't to encourage you to keep it. You probably won't lose it; in fact your relationship with your boss and your co-workers will probably improve if you confront them. But even if there is a risk you will lose it, be aware of the costs of hanging on to it. Usually, what happens is you get a lifeless, depressing job and an unhappy family life for your effort. Eventually, even that trade-off doesn't work. We have an oversupply of cowards with lousy, dead, depressing jobs and lousy, dead, depressing family lives. We don't need any more. Don't volunteer for that job. Damaged heroes with misdirected courage abound.

I have coached a lot of people through conflicts at work in private industry and the government, and many of my clients have climbed to the top of their professions. What seems clear to me is that people don't often advance by simply hoping and behaving themselves. A lot of people waste their time being well-behaved employees, avoiding the risk of telling the truth about resentment, hoping for advancement. The people who actually get to the top are both more nasty and more loving. They are *not* good little passive-aggressive ass-kissers. They are more likely to be ass-kickers. Maybe some of them got kicked upstairs because more passive people couldn't stand putting up with them anymore. Some got promoted because they stopped being willing to stand around and gossip about who was to blame for their unhappiness. By not expressing resentment directly, many people bring about the result they were trying to avoid in the first place — they stay stuck or lose their jobs. Through carefulness and politeness and good behavior, they choke themselves down to being bored, burdensome, stressed out, miserable assholes nobody wants to be around. Unless they are civil servants, some of these people do lose their jobs. Some remain working for the government as paperweights.

Will Telling the Truth about Anger Destroy Our Relationship?

Many of us won't express anger with a loved one. We believe that if we expressed our resentment, it would destroy our relationship and our beloved would leave us. But without the freedom to tell the truth about our experience, our relationships inevitably suffer. When we express only our appreciation and withhold our anger, we lose our ability to *be fully present* with the ones we love, and, sooner or later, we become less able to appreciate them. This is often why relationships end and families break up. Repressing anger to control other people's behavior (in this case, to keep them from leaving) is ultimately what leads to our inability to make contact with them. Repressed anger blocks the flow of love and creativity that we once experienced around them, and generates a flurry of thoughts for us to get caught up in. The more we are caught up in our thoughts, the less present we are to the other person and to what is happening in our own moment-to-moment experience.

Once you start getting more honest with yourself about your judgmental, angry mind, you find yourself confronting this question: "How can I express my resentment in such a way that I strengthen, rather than destroy, my relationships with others?"

There are ways of expressing anger that work, and there are ways of expressing anger that make the situation worse. The ways that work make things worse for a while and better later. These are the ones you want. Most people express anger ineffectively, and then, when they see how uncomfortable the situation has become, decide that it's best to leave those feelings hidden. Their conclusion is incorrect. It is best to learn how to fight so that the air between you and the other person is cleared. When you have "cleared the air," you are free to relate in a brand-new way to that *person* rather than to your *ideas about the person.*

My Anger is Too Explosive; I Might Hurt Someone

In the beginning, an attempt to change the habit of smothering anger can be explosive. The backed-up fund of resentment is released in a torrent.

The first blow-up seems like a nuclear explosion, both because of its magnitude and because it contrasts so dramatically with former politeness. After a little practice, the explosions become like conventional bombs, then like dynamite, and then like firecrackers. The eventual goal is to have hundreds of tiny explosions a minute, like an internal combustion engine. This anger is good fuel to burn; it's what makes Sammy run.

What usually happens without a good guide through the initial explosive experiences is that the person runs away from the experience. For this reason, the progression down the path from "explosion" to "engine" doesn't occur. If a therapist or friend can support an angry person to stay with the experience of being angry even a few seconds longer with each explosion, the cure for phony heroics can begin. *Paying attention to the experience of feeling in the body while angry is the key to learning how to use anger rather than have anger use you.* That awareness of feeling in the body is what causes anger to change from a destructive force to a usable power.

Phony Explosiveness

One has to look and listen carefully to distinguish between a phony expression of anger and an authentic one. A noisy expression of anger is also not always the truth. The over-expression of anger can also be a form of lying, or a way of covering over other feelings, like grief. Some loud-mouthed bastards are angry all the time and loud and intimidating about it to cover over other feelings. This cover-up anger, even though intensely expressed, never decreases or subsides because it is a phony expression in the first place, usually hiding grief or hurt feelings or fear of intimacy.

Experimental and Experiential Approach to Curing Anger Sickness
Look into your own experience of what happens to you when you get angry. Think of someone with whom you are presently angry. If you can't think of anyone, then think of someone whom you don't particularly like. What is it that you don't like about that person? Perhaps you feel that this person is a snob or pushy or dishonest or crude or insensitive. If you contacted that person and told him forthrightly what you didn't like about him and quit there, chances are it would *not* improve your relationship. Don't stop with that. The purpose of expressing your anger directly instead of indirectly is to get in touch with the source of your own judgments. By the time a person decides that he doesn't like someone, he is already one step removed from his anger. When asked if we are angry, many of us manifest this being-removed-from the anger, saying, "I'm not angry, I just don't like him (her) very much," or "I just don't feel he's the kind of person that I want to be around." But these judgments are founded on one or more very specific incidents about which we were angry at one time. We may not be consciously lying, because we may not be experiencing that anger right now. The *form* the anger presently takes is that of judgments, evaluations, and other thoughts. The specific incident may be hard to recall at first, but invariably, judgments

are based on something that the person specifically said or did that we resented. It's not that the person necessarily said or did anything obviously offensive. Maybe she just said "hello" and you didn't like the way she said it. Perhaps what he did reminded you of someone else. The rightness or wrongness of what she said or did is irrelevant.

Your anger is unreasonable and unfair. Let it stay that way. Trying to make it seem reasonable — trying to make the resented person *wrong* — is the source of all the judgments. Strained relations between people are not based on evaluation, "vibes," or "not liking the way they are" as much as on specific events — what they at one time said or did. The evaluations, dislike, and explanations come later. When you can identify what these specific things are, you are in a better position to express your resentment and heal your relationship with that person. We are all more petty and selfish than we are willing to admit. When we are willing to admit our petty anger, we get over it faster and we have less of it in the future.

The process of forgiveness involves the following six minimal requirements, none of which may be skipped.

1. You have to tell the truth about what specific behavior you resent, to the person, face-to-face;

2. You have to be verbally and vocally unrestrained with regard to volume and propriety;

3. You have to pay attention to the feelings and sensations in your body and to the other person *as you speak;*

4. You have to express any appreciations for the person that come up in the process, with the same attention to your feelings and to the other person as when you are expressing resentments;

5. You have to stay with any feelings that emerge in the process, like tears or laughter, regardless of any evaluations you may have about how it makes you look;

6. You have to stay with the discussion until you no longer feel resentful of the other person.

Then, and only then, are you ready to talk about the future, make arrangements for the future, or make any agreements. Any lawyer, priest, psychotherapist, or other patrolman who tells you differently about this is full of shit. Any diplomat, bureaucrat, democrat, labor leader, company executive, head of government, husband, wife, son, or daughter who attempts to do other than this is likewise full of shit.

Exercises for Getting Into and Getting Over Anger

Exercise One. Close your eyes for a moment, picture a person you don't like, and have an imaginary dialogue with him. Tell him your judgments about him. Tell him what he did that you resent. Then imagine his response and respond back. Pay attention to your body as you engage in this imaginary dialogue. Take a break from reading here and do this exercise.

Exercise Two. Go call that person you just had an imaginary conversation with and make an appointment to tell him your resentments in person. (You may also tell him your appreciations if you have any or if any show up after your expression of resentment.) Tell the person when you call that you want to meet him to tell him what you are mad about and get over it, and get complete with him. Ask him to meet with you as a favor to you. Persist until he agrees to meet with you.

Exercise Three. Meet your enemy and forgive her or him, not as a favor to her or him, but for your own selfish benefit. Finish reading this chapter before you go to your meeting.

You Are Probably A Coward

You probably didn't do all three of those exercises. Maybe you never will. Now you know why most cowards like to think of themselves as heroes. They do it to hide; they are too afraid of other people to tell them the truth. They would rather be kind to their enemies than forgive them because it *requires little courage to fake kindness;* it's easier, less risky, less threatening, and less trouble. Don't worry. You are normal.

Most people are too chickenshit to take a stand on telling the truth. In fact, you can start there. Admit it. Tell people. Admit your cowardice — your unwillingness to tell the truth if anything that you judge to be significant is at stake. You lie like hell when you are scared, and you are scared whenever you are angry. Admit it. It's a start.

Guidelines for Expressing Anger

Just in case you decide to grow beyond being normal, here are some guidelines for you to follow in expressing anger. Reading these guidelines will do you no good if you are unwilling to experiment with this approach to see what will happen. This approach does not "make sense." It works experientially. That is, if you try it to see what it feels like, you may get the experience of forgiving the person you were mad at. You may have to experiment with it several times before you get used to the process. It does work, even though it may not make sense.

These guidelines are not moral rules to be memorized and obeyed. They are rules of thumb. The purpose of these guidelines is to direct your attention to the process of learning how to express yourself in the moment so that something happens to actual feelings in your body at the level of sensation. Something will happen because of your willingness to pay attention to your experience. These guidelines will make you aware of your moment-to-moment experience of anger or of appreciation. They are for you to be able to discover something about the process of expression itself.

The rules can be followed and still not work if you are only attending to the rules and not to your experience. The point is to be aware of your experience while experimenting, not whether you are "good" at following the rules.

Your goal is to be willing and able to acknowledge to yourself, and to report to the person with whom you are speaking, each new experience as it emerges, whether or not it is comfortable. If you refuse to quit, and keep talking to the person you're interacting with until you *feel* complete, you will eventually be complete with him. You'll have no more withheld resentments or appreciations, and you'll be able to experience him newly, as he is, in that moment.

Love is when you let someone be the way she is. When you let up on your judgments of someone, there is a free space in which forgiveness and love occur. Here are the guidelines:

◆ *Whenever possible, talk face-to-face to the person with whom you are angry.* It is impossible to do any of this work over the phone. The quality of the interaction is different. You need to look each other in the eye and react to each other moment-to-moment. Over the phone, your contact with the other person is much too limited and you are relating to your concept of him, not to your experience of him as he is. You will miss many of his nonverbal responses. Take the time to see him in person. If he is a long distance away, a phone call is better than nothing, because it can start the process of experiencing the feelings. But don't engage in long conversations on the telephone. To do so is usually a waste of time that increases judgments and displaces feeling. This is the reverse of what is needed when you're mad.

◆ *Start your sentences as often as possible with the words, "I resent you for..." or "I appreciate you for...."* The structure of a sentence that starts with those words ensures that the anger or appreciation is personal, that there is an "I" and a "thou." "I resent you" has a much stronger and more personal impact than "I resent the fact that..." In the latter statement you are saying that you are angry at some "fact." The slight difference in the wording may seem insignificant to you; it is not. Most people resist saying, "I resent you for..." because they don't want to get "personal." They are uncomfortable when they are directly expressing their resentment to someone.

While it is more comfortable to be less direct and say, "I resent it when...," it won't work. You won't be able to completely experience your resentment and have it disappear unless you are willing to tell the truth. You resent people, not facts or vague "its." Neither will it work to substitute something milder for the word "resent." "I am annoyed at you for..." and "I am angry with you about..." are introductions to a story *about* anger. Those phrases deal more with a general description of a state of being than with the *active* expression of anger. "I resent you" is different in that it is active and transitive, something you are feeling toward another person in the present moment of speaking while the person is there. If doing this makes you uncomfortable, fine. If you expect to handle your resentment without discomfort, given how you were raised, you can forget it. Make yourself uncomfortable on purpose. Acting according to what feels comfortable when you are attempting to get over anger is a mistake. It's like drinking Pepto-Bismol to keep from vomiting, staying sick for three hours, and then puking your guts up anyway.

A lot of people are also uncomfortable expressing direct appreciation and have as much difficulty admitting warmth as anger. Appreciations often emerge right in the middle of expressing resentment. Appreciations are to be handled in the same way and gotten over in the same way. Trying to hold on to appreciation works just as poorly as trying to avoid resentment. New appreciation for a person can only emerge in a clearing created by completing the experience of past appreciations and resentments.

◆ *Speak in the present tense.* Just because you are talking about something he did in the past, don't say, "I resented you." You still resent that person, right now, for what he did or said in the past, so state it in the present tense. In the past tense, resentments are only descriptions or stories about what happened or how you were. They won't change the nature of your relationship — of how you are now. When resentments are stated in the present tense, you get the chance to feel angry again and to experience the anger. When you can experience the feeling, it disappears. As I have said over and over, when you avoid the experience of anger, it persists in the form of apparently reasonable thoughts. The thoughts are poisonous and not constructive. They are destructive, because they distance you from the other person. They allow you to avoid contact with the other person and your experience and to maintain your righteousness rather than express the anger and get off of your pose.

◆ *Eventually, get specific.* Even though it doesn't always feel this way, you probably resent the person for what he specifically did or said. For example, if you say to someone, "I resent you for being a snob," or "I resent you for acting snobbish toward me," he won't be clear about what you resent — although he may imagine he is clear about it. He'll probably just say, "I'm not a snob." You haven't told him what he actually did or said that you resented — what led you to the conclusion that he was snobbish. You are demanding that the person "buy in" to your judgment of him. You might begin by expressing a judgment, but you must eventually get specific. If you haven't gotten down to the specifics yet, you aren't finished. Look closer into what the person actually did that made you conclude that he was snobbish, and say that. In this example, the real resentment might be expressed by, "I resent you for turning your head and not answering me when I said "Hi" to you at the grocery store." Or, "I resent you for saying 'only hicks like country music' the other day."

◆ *Don't stop with general descriptions of behavior or general judgments.* When you throw in the words "always" or "never," the person won't get what you're talking about and you won't get over the resentment. He doesn't have to get it. It isn't true. He hears only that you're trying to make him wrong. "I resent you for constantly complaining," isn't specific. Report the specific incident(s) that you remember: "I resent you for saying I bought the wrong groceries last Thursday, and I resent you for saying 'I *guess* I'll *have to* buy groceries' yesterday." Similarly, "I resent you for never appreciating me," or "I resent you for not being romantic," are both too vague and too global to be gotten over. Remember you are doing this to get over your grudge, rather than to provide a case against your enemy. This resentment must be expressed more specifically, such as, "I resent you for getting drunk and falling asleep on our anniversary."

If you are too mad, at first, to interrupt your own mind by being more specific, go ahead and be general, but do it as loudly as possible. What you get from intensity will compensate, in the beginning, for what you lack in specificity. Just remember to go back over the same ground in a more specific way after you blow out the vents.

◆ *Focus as much as you can on what did happen instead of what didn't happen.* When you resent someone for what he didn't do — that is, violating your expectations — look back to what he said or did to create that expectation. Express your resentment to him for what he said or did. Lousy as it may seem, you are the only one who is responsible for all of your expectations, disappointment, and anger. You can, however, get over the misery you create for yourself by expressing your anger out loud, instead of living in a little hut of poison thoughts.

◆ *Stay in touch with your experience as you talk.* If you just present someone with a rehearsed, carefully-worded statement about your resentment, you probably won't have much of an experience of your anger dissipating. It's important to express your feelings as they come up during the interaction. For instance, suppose your spouse reminds you of an obligation and you get mad. You might say, "I resent you for asking me if I remembered to get Grandma a birthday present." You probably already felt guilty about forgetting Grandma's present. You resent your spouse for asking you the question. When you pursue the experience further, you may resent your spouse for telling you to get a present in the first place. You may resent Grandma for having a birthday. You may resent having a grandmother, having to buy her a present, being told to get her a present, being asked if you got it, the tone of voice of the questioner, the look on the face of the questioner, the smell in the room when the question was asked. You may resent the clerk at the store where you went for the present, who said they were out of Grandma's brand. What you need to do to tell the truth and have the resentment disappear is this: first, notice the bodily sensations associated with what you have called guilt (feeling constricted in your breathing, cowering, feeling tense, frowning) and state your resentment clearly. Start with, "I resent you for saying, 'Did you remember to get something for Grandma for her birthday?' " Then, "I resent you for your innocent, phony tone of voice" (abstract). "I resent you for your tone of voice when you asked me that question" (more specific). "I resent you for looking at me now." "I resent you for frowning." "I resent you for mentioning Grandma at all." This may sound ridiculous and unfair. Clearly your spouse is not at fault and is being blamed. But note this: the unfair blaming is being done out loud. It is in the public domain where it can get cleared up, not in your secretive mind. People outside of you can be depended on to fight back and take care of themselves. You can depend on it. You don't need to protect your spouse from your irrationality. You will get set straight in a minute. Try it. What you want is the feeling of completion and wholeness that comes when you have told the truth about your petty, selfish mind and raised hell out loud like a fool. What a relief! You don't have to feel guilty now. You and your spouse now live in a new space.

You may have some withheld appreciation to express as well. You can appreciate someone for the same thing you resented her for, and often do. You and Grandma can also have a more alive relationship if you tell each other the truth about your anger and guilt and sense of obligation. Go see Grandma and tell her the truth. What you put out there relieves you. What you withhold will kill you.

◆ *Stay there with the person beyond the time it takes to exchange resentments.* If you are willing to state your resentments, and keep stating them as they come up, and allow the other person to resent you for resenting him, eventually you won't have anything left to resent each other for. At that point, you're still not finished. If you can't think of how to end the sentence, "I appreciate you for...," it may mean that you are still angry and that you haven't finished expressing your resentments — so keep going. Don't rush to forgive someone out of being uncomfortable about having so many resentments. Be honest about whether or not you really feel complete with the person. Be willing to have it take as long as it takes. It probably won't take as long as you fear. It will probably take longer than you like.

◆ *After you both have fully expressed your specific resentments, state your appreciation the same way.* Say, "I appreciate you for..." not "I appreciate the fact that...." Keep checking your body to see how you feel. Are your shoulders tense? Do you feel relaxed? Do you feel like you want to get away from this situation as soon as possible? If the latter is true, there is more that you are withholding. Tell the truth of your experience even if it's, "I still feel uncomfortable sitting here with you," or "I appreciate you for staying here and listening to me." When you feel warmth in your chest and a smile on your face, express your appreciation in a clear way: "I appreciate you for the way you look right now," or "I appreciate you for agreeing to do this experiment with me." After some appreciations are expressed some more resentments may emerge. If that happens, express those resentments and go on. Eventually you will just be sitting in a room looking at a person. You will see clearer. You will be willing to live and let live. You will be grateful to her for having stuck with you through another fight.

◆ *Keep it up.* After an emotional exchange in which two people tell the truth, they often retreat into superficiality. People notice that even though they felt loving and inspired after they talked, weeks may go by before they see each other again. This is not an accident. After we release our withheld anger, we discover our appreciation. More often than not we realize that we really love this person. People are scared of feeling anger, but they are terrified of experiencing love. It's no wonder that when an authentic exchange occurs, the next time the two people meet, they will talk about anything but their real feelings. One may say as an aside, "You know, I'm so glad we had that talk last time. It meant so much to me." Then they'll switch the subject to something trivial. Once you have broken through to another person by telling the truth, you have an incredible opportunity to have a real, alive relationship. The two of you can support each other to continue to tell the truth. It takes practice. You will tend to withhold your feelings on later occasions because you have practiced that for years, but you can always clean it up with the person as soon as you realize that you are withholding.

Exercises Again

The steps to diminish both the amount of anger you have and the degree to which that anger runs your life are these: *1.* transform your relationship to anger by agreement; and *2.* change your experience of anger through awareness. Awareness is what causes change, not a moral resolve to be better.

A little earlier in this chapter I gave you some exercises and you probably chickened out. Here is another chance. These exercises are just suggestions. You don't have to do them and they may be useful just at certain times when you are stuck with how to get over your anger.

Agreement to Experiment with Anger

Get with some friends or your spouse and members of your family old enough to read this chapter. Read this chapter. Meet afterward and make an agreement to experiment for ten days with telling the truth about your resentments to each other, as a method of support for each other. Agree that for ten days, all resentments may legitimately be expressed. That doesn't mean they all have to be acted on. For example, if one of you says, "I resent you for parking in front of the driveway and I demand that you move your car," the offender doesn't have to move the car. All he has to do is hear the resentment. When the going gets rough, if it does, keep in mind that the exercise is to go on for ten days.

Have a Conversation in a Group About Anger

Get a group of friends together and start an ongoing group to support each other for a while in learning about how to handle anger. Start by asking them to read this chapter and talk about it in the group.

Ask for Help from Friends

If you are stuck at not being able to make the arrangements to meet someone to express and get over your anger, because you are too cowardly or the person won't meet with you, or if you get stuck during the meeting, ask a third party in. Get a mutual friend to mediate. Ask both of your friends, the one you resent and the one you asked to help, to read this chapter.

Further Exercises

For further exercises, read John O. Stevens' book, *Awareness: Exploring, Experimenting, Experiencing*[2], particularly the three exercises entitled *Guilt, Resentment,* and *Demand.*

Guilt

Those situations in all of our lives where we feel that terrible feeling of having done something bad and been caught, of having made a real mistake and feeling bad about it, don't seem to be related to anger at all. You just feel bad. When you feel your way through the experience by facing it, anger will show up, and your power to get over the guilt comes from facing every detail and every imagined catastrophe.

Anger shows up when you examine your guilt feelingly, because guilt, when it was first learned, came from instances of what Fritz Perls called "projected resentment." When you were a child, you were powerless, and you sometimes got mad at the adults who made you do some things and wouldn't let you do other things. When you were mad at them and you made a mistake you knew they would get you for, you felt very bad. If you were mad at the big person who was going to be mad at you, and you had to deny your anger or else make things even worse, you felt even guiltier. You imagined they would be very mad at you, based on denying that you were mad at them, and as an attempt to keep them from punishing you too bad, you punished yourself. If you were hard enough on yourself, you might have escaped some of their wrath, and if you learned to control your terrible self so your anger toward them didn't show, you might likewise have avoided their wrath. Better to be punished by yourself than by them.

So when you feel guilty, check to see if some of the anger you imagine on the part of the offended party is, in fact, your anger toward them. Mistakes are often made in the first place out of anger. People who are perennial fuck-ups are usually angry people.

Meditation

If you are willing to confront your anger in all the ways I have discussed, and if you are *not* using meditation to avoid acknowledging and expressing anger, then meditation works. Meditation can increase your satisfaction and decrease your anger. If you want your anger to decrease noticeably in a relatively short time, and if you are willing to do all of what I have discussed so far, meditate regularly. You will gradually become noticeably less angry as who you consider yourself to be changes to include your experience of just sitting quietly. You will become more familiar with yourself as the *noticer.* You will gradually become less attached to yourself as a personality. I recommend Transcendental Meditation. TM instructors are great at teaching meditation. (Don't take any of their advice about anger.)

Review and Summary

These exercises and guidelines for expressing resentment and appreciation are for your use in discovering how to let the experience of anger work itself out. These rules of thumb are suggested as substitutes for your usual methods of controlling anger. They are intended to assist you to experience your anger more intensely and publicly so you will have a better chance of getting over being angry. You may get angry at me because, after following the guidelines, you will feel like you are more angry than you used to be. When this occurs, consider the possibility that you are not angrier but are simply experiencing anger more. Then see for yourself if you get a result that works better than your former methods of control. If not, you don't get your money back.

Here is a quick review of the rules of thumb about anger:

◆ Whenever possible, talk face-to-face to the person with whom you are angry.

◆ Start your sentences as often as possible with the words, "I resent you for..." or "I appreciate you for...."

◆ Speak in the present tense.

◆ Eventually, get specific.

◆ Don't stop with general descriptions of behavior or general judgments.

◆ Focus as much as you can on what did happen instead of what didn't happen.

◆ Stay in touch with your experience as you talk.

◆ Stay there with the person beyond the time it takes to exchange resentments.

◆ After you both have fully expressed your specific resentments, state your appreciations the same way.

◆ Keep it up.

Why Do All of This?

Being honest about anger puts you on the road back home to being alive like you were as a child instead of mind-deadened by what you have learned to lie about. Telling the truth about your anger is a way to get back to your experience of being, where you love yourself and therefore have something left over with which to love someone else. Revealing the withheld judgments and feelings you have hidden, out of politeness and your protection racket, is the difference between a life lived in hate and a life lived in love. Coming forth with your anger will give you your life back. It is a way to feel complete and not be in need of someone else to make you be whole. It is one of the ways back to the path of the "light that enlightens the light," that light of being that first clicked on in the womb and which still is humming right along now, even as we speak.

That is one reason. Here is one more.

There are 51,500 nuclear warheads armed and at the ready, still, right now, after the Reagan-Gorbachev talks and the Bush-Gorbachev agreements have made us all feel better. 25,000 of them belong to the United States, 25,000 to the Soviet Union, and 1,500 are spread among other countries. Many of them are capable of unleashing 10 to 20 times the destructive power dropped on Hiroshima. They are sitting there, waiting for some family argument, or for some righteous excuse, or for some computer programmer to get pissed off. ✐

TELLING THE TRUTH IN A COUPLE

"I've been too long in the wind, too long in the rain,
taking any comfort that I can
Looking back in longing for the freedom of my chains,
lying in your loving arms again."
— from "Loving Arms" by Tom Jans

THERE IS SOMETHING LOST and something gained in coupling up. You give away a lot of power and freedom when you get in a relationship. I had a few times between marriages when I could do any goddamned thing I wanted to, without having to account to some woman for it. Every time, after a while, I traded my freedom in for the greater act of creation and the other form of freedom of a committed relationship.

I am greatly prejudiced in the direction of the benefits of a committed relationship exceeding the deficits, partly because I don't think you can beat loving and being loved by a child — even though when you have children, your entire life gets organized around them and limited for a lot of years. There are also great advantages in sharing the work of survival with another person.

I have been married four times. The most recent, now that I

am older and have learned more, has been the most successful. My current wife Amy and I have been together for fourteen years. Through the generosity of her opening to me over and over again, I have been learning to practice what I preach. Her unwillingness to be any category I have for her and her willingness to engage with me in the "Great Conversation," her listening to what I say and hearing it sometimes clearer than how I speak it, and her acts of co-creation with me have helped me stay awake and alive. Our conscious, committed interest in the Great Conversation, the three-thousand-year-old ongoing dialogue of Western Civilization, is a vital background of our relationship to each other. A second vital background is our dependable mutual commitment to telling the truth. We are not willing to kiss anybody's ass by lying to them, including each others'.

This relationship with Amy has been a voluntary imprisonment in growing. The best things we have done together, like having our little girl, Carson, and helping raise my daughter, Shanti, and my son, Amos, from childhood to adolescence, and raising my two nephews, Zeke and Casey, and maintaining a house and budget and jobs to pay for them, and building a house where we now live in the mountains, and a few other things, are things I couldn't have done without her. She couldn't have done these things without me either. Each of us is a powerful person in our own right because of our separate commitments to learning, training, growing, and creating our lives, because of having each other to learn from, and because of a lot of other couples from whom we have both learned.

We have participated in a lot of trainings together, and conducted a lot of couples groups and trainings ourselves. I don't know how other folks who don't do this kind of work on themselves can stand staying together. Actually, I do know how they do it, and sometimes it's not a pretty sight.

Amy and I lived together for six years before we got married and now we have been married for eight years. Getting along together has not all been rosy. We got mad and split up a few times, but the separations never lasted more than a few days.

Living together in close proximity is one of the toughest things human beings can do. Over half of the people who get married in this country get divorced. Of the remaining 47% or so who stay together, I imagine at least half are angry, co-dependent, dead unions based on fear, lethargy, and shame. These people live together in a kind of variable form of ongoing pain somewhere between divorce and the emergency room.

Of the 25% remaining, my guess is that maybe half are passive, intellectual space-cadet compromises of the sort that make up your standard middle class survival system: the socially acceptable dysfunctional family. It seems a little extravagant to say that 12 1/2% of the couples that pair up have good, alive, intimate, honest, functional relationships, but what the hell, I'm feeling generous. This cheery information is not based on science but is informed speculation on my part. Regardless of the accuracy of my estimates on how many relationships are successful, I can make a few recommendations and give examples of what can help.

A Checklist for Intimacy

If you are in a couple and you are reading this chapter with an eye to having it help you have a better relationship with your mate, God bless you, I hope this works. If you are willing to risk and want to grow together, start by using the following checklist for intimacy, and if you haven't done a particular item on the list with your mate, do it.

1. Tell each other your entire life story, taking about 3 hours each.

2. Tell each other your complete sexual history, including how many people you have had sex with, what gender they were and the details of what you did with them.

3. Masturbate to orgasm in front of each other with no assistance from each other.

4. Tell each other of any affairs, near-affairs, necking, arousal, daydream or flirtation you have engaged in since you have known each other.

5. Take turns with a half-hour monologue in which one of you agrees to be silent for 30 minutes while the other speaks. Tell your partner everything you resent them for and everything you appreciate them for. After you have both taken a turn, talk about the two monologues for at least a half an hour.

Whichever of the above you haven't done that you least want to do, do first, with one exception: the last recommendation, taking turns at monologues of appreciation and resentment, should be done last, after all the others are complete. When you do this exercise, refer to the previous chapter, HOW TO DEAL WITH ANGER, because you will have to work out a way to handle anger to make your relationship work for both of you. Anger will come up and must be handled if you are to make it as a growing couple. Anger is never permanently handled. If it isn't stockpiled, you have handled it the best it can be handled. If you work through what has been previously hidden or withheld and any appreciation or resentment associated with it so that you forgive each other, you have a new beginning. New beginnings are the secret to success in committed relationships.

Telling the Truth About Sex

I am still amazed at how normally intelligent people who have been living together or married and having sex for years still can't talk to each other about fucking. Most couples haven't told each other about their sexual *history,* much less their current sexual involvements. According to a recent survey by James Patterson and Peter Kim reported in their book, *The Day America Told the Truth*[1], 35% of married people are having an affair and keeping it secret from their spouses.

There are three areas of conversation about sex: sexual history, sex with each other, and current sexual activities or interests other than the partner. It is important to cover all of these bases. It is even more important to speak at a descriptive level of conversation rather than an abstract level. Whether you are talking about the past or a recent involvement, be graphic about what happened. Don't just say "I went to bed with Martha;" say: "Martha and I spent all of Friday night in bed. We fucked three times. She gave me a blow job. I ate her and she came. We giggled and drank wine and talked. We cuddled a lot and we had a great time. We really loved each other." After such a report, answer any questions your mate has about what went on and what you felt and what the other person said or did. Anything less than full disclosure is withholding of the kind that creates alienation. There is no such thing as "none of your business" in an intimate relationship.

Sexual History

Start out by telling your sexual history in detail with regard to what happened and what you felt physically and emotionally. Tell about what age you were when you first had sex, what you thought about sex, how it felt, and how you felt about it, how it felt when you first had an orgasm, when you first masturbated on purpose, when you first had sex with any other being. Tell all your techniques, fantasies, and methods of seduction. Speak at a descriptive level and go back through the experiences by reliving them as you tell them so more detail emerges.

Sex with Each Other

Demonstrate whatever pleases you that you have the power to demonstrate. Touch yourself in the ways you like to be touched and describe what you are doing while you do it. Have your partner practice touching you in the ways you like, and say what you don't like. It is your responsibility to train your partner to please you. This is simply a matter of an adult human being taking good care of himself or herself. I frequently prescribe the exercise, included in the previous list, of masturbating to orgasm in front of each other with no assistance from each other. This exercise is useful in several ways. Not only do people get a chance to demonstrate being pleased sexually and how they do it for themselves, they also demonstrate, for the benefit of their partner, their capability to please themselves without help. That relieves a sense of obligation for taking care of each other sexually and opens up an area of permission to play. As in other areas of life, when people don't feel like they *have* to perform, they are free to perform. There is no reason why both people in a partnership can't have orgasms every time they have sex. If one partner takes longer to come than another, instead of having an argument about who comes too early and who comes too late, get a vibrator or some pornographic books or tapes and work on a way of both coming each time whether simultaneously or not. When you don't say and do what you want, don't blame your partner.

Sex with Other People

Tell your partner about people that show up in your life that you get the hots for. Share fantasies out loud about sex with these people. You can share your turn-ons to other people with each other and have a lot of fun with it. You can do this whether you actually have sex with other people or not. If you do have sex with other people together or separately, be sure to tell each other what it was like for you and how you felt and feel about the other person. Be sure this description is in great detail and remains current. *Whether you are monogamous or polygamous is not the most critical factor in having a successful couple. Whether or not you tell the truth is.* Whatever your agreements about who or when you can fuck, tell the truth about who you do fuck, who you want to fuck, and how it is when you fuck them or daydream about it.

[183]

The more uncompromising you are about sharing, as a stand, whether it shocks or hurts or offends your partner or not, the better chance you have for a powerful relationship.

Powerful Relationships

In powerful relationships, our nature as human beings is revealed to us. The fundamental way we come to know who we are is in relationships. Martin Buber has the following to say about our nature as human beings:

> The world is twofold for man in accordance with his twofold attitude.
>
> The attitude of man is twofold in accordance with the two basic words he can speak.
>
> The basic words are not single words but word pairs.
>
> One basic word is the word pair I-You.
>
> The other basic word is the word pair I-It; but this basic word is not changed when He or She takes the place of It.
>
> Thus the I of man is also twofold.
>
> For the I of the basic word I-You is different from that in the basic word I-It.

≈ ≈ ≈

> Basic words do not state something that might exist outside them; by being spoken they establish a mode of existence.
>
> Basic words are spoken with one's being.
>
> When one says You, the I of the word pair I-You is

said, too.

When one says It, the I of the word pair I-It is said, too.

The basic word I-You can only be spoken with one's whole being.

The basic word I-It can never be spoken with one's whole being.[2]

When you use the word "I" to refer to yourself, you are referring either to yourself as defined by relation to an It, or yourself as defined by relating to a You. "I" doesn't always mean the same thing. Sometimes "I" refers to one self and sometimes "I" refers to another, entirely different self. When you are a being, standing before another being, you are a different being than when you are a being standing before an it, an idea, or a thing, that is not a being. We are all in the habit of using the word "I," as though it always means the same thing or points to the same referent.

Ask yourself when you are talking to your partner, "Am I relating to a Being or to a category?" Which would you rather be, a person relating to a being with PMS, or a person relating to PMS? Would you rather relate to a being who is slightly inebriated, or to a goddamned drunk you know of old? Who are you being, what kind of person are you being, how are you different one time than you are at another?

When we Gestalt therapists recommend that you use the phrase, "I resent You for!" or "I appreciate You for!," we are not as dumb as we sound. The assertion, "I resent You for!" is a statement of a feeling expressed by one being related to another being. Because the being is present to and willing to experience the feeling in the presence of the other, there is a chance that the experience, not suppressed but expressed, can come and go. In its place is a new opening to the other. Likewise, when "I appreciate You!" is expressed, the feeling of appreciation can come and go, leaving a new opening for love that is much deeper than the bullshit romanticism that passes for love on soap operas. When "I-You" is spoken with an active, transitive, present tense verb (resent, appreciate) between the I and the You, denoting a present feeling, the moment's truth is spoken in its entirety. Then the truth changes. *When the truth changes from your speaking, you know you've spoken the truth.*

So at any given time, when two people are relating, for each of them there are two possible kinds of "I's" and two possible kinds of "You's," namely: "I-You" I, "I-It" I, and "I-You" you, and "I-It" you. When "I-You" I speaks to "I-You" you, we both are on the same page, and communication occurs. When "I-You" I speaks to "I-It" you, we aren't on the same page, but there is a chance for a breakthrough for you to the world of being from the world of categorization, *i.e.,* a chance for deliverance from your mind. When "I-It" I speaks to "I-You" you, there is a chance for a breakthrough to the world of being for me. When "I-It" I speaks to "I-It" you, we are on the same page, and we are in an interminable fucking fight.

<u>I</u>   <u>YOU</u>

I-You →   I-You
    ↘

I-It   I-It

I can relate to you as a
thing or a being

The problem with all of this is, when we are mad at someone, the first thing we want to do to punish him is to cut him off
by turning him into a category, which then gives us a chance to
have an orgasm of righteous indignation. This is fairly gratifying,
but leaves you hungry and empty in a strange way. You get a hit
of righteous energy, but you do not have a powerful relationship.
However, if you are committed to the rediscovery of being, in
your partner and yourself, there is a pretty good chance you can
have a powerful loving relationship, where forgiveness and renewal occur over and over again, and you feel full. Once you
both get a taste of this you won't want to quit.

Couples who come to see me in therapy are usually pissed off
at each other and out for revenge, both primarily looking for a
therapist to support them in making their partner wrong. They
are two "I-It"'s in an interminable fight. Each one of them usually says, in one form or another, pointing to his or her partner,
"Tell It to leave me alone."

How Relationships Develop from Intimacy to Hatred
I work with single people who have been trying to find a mate for

years and who want my coaching so they can get married. I end up going to a number of weddings every year and help conduct some of them. I talk about the following distinctions:

1. *Intimacy is not the same thing as romance.*

Being "in Love" at the beginning of a relationship is wonderful. I think it is the result of us getting in touch with being, through another person. When you fall in love and get in that blissful state, you just love being, your being and the being of the beloved and the being of all beings in the world. You are "home" in that rediscovered sense of unity and bliss. As Kris Kristofferson sings:

> *She wasn't quite as pretty as some others I have known,*
> *and she wasn't good at conversation when we were alone,*
> *but she had a way of makin' me believe that I belonged.*
> *And it felt like comin' home when I loved her.*

> *'Cause she brightened up my day like the early mornin' sun*
> *and she made what I was doin' seem worth while.*
> *It's the closest thing to livin' that I guess I've ever known,*
> *and it left me feelin' warm, when I loved her.*

It is not the way they look or how good they talk that makes us love who we love. Their ability to be with us is more powerful. It is their ability to make us "believe that we belong," that "leaves us feelin' warm," that renews that old spark that first happened in Mom an eternity ago.

Too bad that once we are warmed, and begin to "believe that we belong," the feeling becomes a *belief*, to be preserved and guarded and defended so the feeling will never go away. This of course, makes the feeling go away.

We end up resenting the person, with whom we used to be in love, for changing. When you start expecting the other person to live up to your expectations based on what you felt before, you are going to get disappointed and pissed off. If both people are in this place at about the same time, a nasty argument ensues. This hurt and anger get formulated into belief instead of gotten over. In a short while, you are trapped in the thought, "How could that bitch/bastard be so wonderful *and* so shitty to me? How can she/he be so cruel?"

Next, after a few of these arguments, the two parties alternate between feeling insecure and feeling angry. When one gets angry the other gets scared he or she is about to be abandoned. This alternating process occurs a few times. Then, a discussion like the following one occurs. (This discussion occurred recently with a couple I was seeing.)

The fellow is in his fifties, has been divorced three times, and is in a new relationship with one of my clients who is being coached on having relationships based on telling the truth. His last lover had walked out on him; he still "loved" her, of course, since she had rejected him.

"I really like you," he said. "These six weeks since we met have been just great. I have never told anyone so much, or had such an honest relationship. I thought, in the beginning, there would be all kinds of bells and whistles. But there aren't any bells or whistles or rockets going off. I have dreaded this conversation for a few days now. I think you are more involved with me than

I with you. I am not in love with you. We have great sex. We laugh together all the time. But I'm not 'in love' like I have experienced before. And since we have been so honest about everything else I think we have to be honest about this."

The woman who was my client had a predictable built-in reaction to this, which was "Oh shit! Here we go again. Why can't I ever have a relationship work out? Just when I was thinking about us moving in together, he wants to back away. This is how it always goes. I am never quite good enough. I am good, but not good enough." As you see, the condition by this time had become two minds relating to each other as Its, coming out of the same mouths that used to be used by their beings for love. They are both right about each other when they say "you changed" because, of course, both have changed. In just six weeks, they have changed from beings out of their mind with love into minded beings.

Half of these wonderful beginnings split up. If they are "like-minded" beings, they stay together in boredom the rest of their lives. If they escape their minds' beliefs about each other repeatedly, they have a successful relationship.

I talked to this particular woman alone, and then to her lover and her together. I suggested that the way they had been telling the truth to each other in the beginning, and even in the moment of our speaking together, was what a powerful relationship is made of. I recalled to him and to myself how badly some of our previous relationships based on romantic love had worked out. I said, "Soap operas are full of people who are in love and start withholding from each other. The nostalgia for what used to be, combined with resentment and hope for renewal, produces what we call romantic love. Romantic love is highly overrated. Romantic love is not as strong as a new friendship based on telling the truth. Romantic love is still fun, though not as romantic, without the tragic overtones of soap opera that come from withholding and being secretive. Romantic love recurs, every now and then, rather than dying after the honeymoon is over, if people have open-to-each-other relationships. Keep working on telling the truth about everything that goes on with each of you and you can work your way through to a powerful relationship." That was my stand, and the place I listened to them from, and though I did my best and so did they, they didn't succeed. Those guys didn't make it. They parted, having learned another increment of information about relationships, but not a sufficient one to allow them to make that one work.

2. Desperation is a terrible basis for union.

If the couple I just talked about had gotten married when they got scared they were about to lose each other, and stayed married on that basis, it would have been a desperate union. That kind of marriage sucks.

3. Loving the holy human prototype is more important than loving the personality.

The holy human prototype is the person you see when you look into someone else's eyes without prejudgment. The holy human prototype is like a child. It is the noticer. It is the being, just like you, just across from you. It is the being who, you can tell by just looking, like looking in a mirror, has the same kind of electric circuitry as yourself. You can love that being of the other as much as you love yourself. When that being is a child, you can love her more than yourself. Beings do a better job of loving each other than minds.

Things That Help Couples Have A Powerful Relationship

↝ *Complete any incomplete relationships with your parental family.* Go have a revealing conversation with your father, mother, brother, sister, or any important earlier relation. This gives you completion as well as practice in renewal. This, along with the work suggested at the beginning of this chapter, helps you finish incomplete situations from the past so you can begin living in the present, being present to each other, and living toward the future.

↝ *Create together some common cause you are both interested in and committed to accomplishing.* This opens up the possibility of working together, in communication with each other, in agreement about what you are both dedicated to accomplishing. You feel helped by each other, grateful to each other, willing to acknowledge each other, and capable of bringing about results in the world together. Actually creating something together is a lot of fun. Babies are fun to create, although they are a hell of a lot of work for a long time. Creating is a lot more fun than bitching and whining.

↝ *Stay involved with other people committed to telling the truth and to something bigger than their own comfort.* An honest relationship with other couples supports your couple. Couples need another couple or two for friends. If intimacy doesn't extend to friends and extended family, the network of support is too thin. If you have even one good friend to both people, to whom both can talk and who supports both in telling the truth, you have a great resource.

    Make requests from your mate for what you want but stay willing to take care of yourself. You can practice this by picking something you usually bitch about your mate's not doing for you, and then sit down with them and practice. You say something like this: "If you want to please me, if you want to know what would make me happy, here is what I would really like for you to do:_____. If you don't do that; it's O.K., I'm a big girl (boy), and I will take care of it myself. You are not obligated to make or keep me happy or to do what I want. I am responsible for my own happiness. If I get mad at you, I will handle it, and I'll get over it. If I get disappointed, I'll be responsible for my own disappointment." Wouldn't it be great to be married to someone who really did that? This is a fine basic sort of position to come from to relate to other people in general: here is what I want, but you don't have to provide it for me. You are invited and requested, but not obligated, to take care of me.

    Take any help you can get. Stay involved with some ongoing context for learning and working on communication. Amy and I have received invaluable support from courses we have taken at Werner Erhard and Associates (now Landmark Educational Foundation).

There are groups of people willing to contribute to other people everywhere there are people. That is one fine thing about which we current humans should all be very happy. Some groups are better at supporting people than others, but the world is full of people who wish to contribute to other people.

᠀ *Grow or die.* If you don't keep growing you go dead.

᠀ *Have a long conversation* (some time when you are *not* arguing) *about when you first got together and how your relationship has evolved over time.* Talk about times of jealousy, times of not much of anything, times of not much sex, times of sex that's not much, times you have worked well together. Talk about how your marriage has been a cauldron. Talk about when you have made the cauldron into a flower pot.

Summary
We are back to the beginning now. Back to the beginning of this book, where we talked about that little being whose life came on in the womb. Back to that little being we go and discover the source of love. Full love, in orgasm, in sleeping together, in cuddling, in cuddling children, is a loss of identity at a time when you know who you are more completely than ever. When you are lost in love, your personality is included in something bigger than itself or else it is obliterated. How lucky can you get? ᠀

PSYCHOTHERAPY: THE JOURNEY FROM MORALISM TO TELLING THE TRUTH

MANY OF THE PEOPLE who go to therapists or physicians seeking relief are tired. They are tired from having worked out their lives in such a way that they get worn out instead of recharged by living. When someone like this takes responsibility for exercise, nutrition, and rest, a number of their "psychological" problems disappear. The human body has a wonderful capacity to restore itself if it is given a break from abuse and a chance to rest.

Wellness is a natural state of being for people who have learned how to get out of their own way. People's health is a result of many factors, including their genetic inheritance, the environment in which they live, their lifestyles, and the health care they receive. Much of the "health care" in our culture has been and still is illness care, aimed at restoring ability to function once it has been lost. We have all learned that this is not good enough, but we are still learning how to maintain good health and prevent disease without moralism crippling the attempt. Sometimes I see people working out or jogging with expressions on their faces that look like their minds are eating them alive at the time. I imagine their suffering for the sake of good health is hard on their health.

A Brief Historical Note

What we consider to be a normal amount of stimulation for an average human being is far greater than what was considered normal during all of previous human history. Quite recently there has been a change in the way humans live. For the greater part of human history, most people lived harder, shorter, and less hyperstimulated lives. Although there were emotional peaks of joy or terror, the average level of stimulation was relatively low. There was time for life to pass through cycles in which tension alternated with periods of rest and regeneration. Life followed the seasons, and the daily cycle of light and dark had a greater influence on how one lived.

After the Industrial Revolution, the tempo of change quickened, and destabilizing new experience became more frequent, the interludes of regeneration shorter. Today we are battered by an endless stream of stimuli, and, for many of us, the unregenerated nervous system remains in a state of persistent tension. Human biochemistry has not adapted to the radical change in lifestyle. Our bodies were not designed to do what we do. As the body's systems organize themselves to respond to the incessant presence of stimulation without reprieve, their flexibility and function begin to be impaired. The impairment in the natural flexibility of the dynamic systems of the body eventually manifests itself as disease. At best, we are open to diseases of overstimulation; at worst, we are victims of serious stress disorders that can kill.

The progression from a normal work/relaxation cycle, to diseases of overstimulation, to stress disorders, can be described like this:

Normal Stimulation and Rest Cycle: There is a balance of tension when appropriate (to do work, to defend against threat, to play) and relaxation (to regenerate energy).

Diseases of Overstimulation without Reprieve: Insomnia, fatigue, jitteriness, inability to relax, inability to concentrate, boredom, "creative blocks," depression, and being overweight are some of the symptoms. The nervous system is stuck in a mild but persistent "fight or flight" tension state. Smooth muscle tissue cannot relax; internal biochemistry has adapted to this state and maintains it.

Stress Disorders: Stress disorders are the logical extension of diseases of overstimulation. These are chronic insomnia, psychosomatic illnesses, high blood pressure, hypertension, paranoid fantasies, hypersensitivity, and death by apoplexy. The machine begins to kill itself, slowly or quickly.

There are a number of different treatment procedures that work effectively to bring about a reduction of stress and a restoration of the natural process of regeneration. We are seeing the dawn of a new era of healing in which physical health and psychological well-being are synonymous. People who are not well psychologically poison and hurt themselves physically. Some of the ways we poison and hurt ourselves are a part of our tradition. (Two of the commonly-accepted forms of treatment for stress are beer and food — the poor person's tranquilizers.)

Stress is most often dealt with only after it has become acute. Only when the unremitting presence of tension is manifest as a disorder or disease do we speculate that perhaps we need to relax. Out of our learned numbness, we allow stress to accumulate, further numbing our innate aliveness. Alcohol and drugs provide a temporary respite from our life-numbing, distracting minds. After the respite from our minds comes the hangover or the letdown. When this form of relief becomes habitual, greater stress is always the result, because people become obsessively attached to some form of relief that is poisonous. This is the vicious cycle of addiction. *Permanent* addiction to *temporary relief* occurs, particularly if drugs or alcohol contrast strongly enough with whatever alternatives people have for relief from their own minds. Entrapment in the ghetto of the mind is a worse alternative than addiction for most addicts, so they stay addicted.

Alcoholism cuts across all classes, because the self-torture of moralism cuts across all classes. One of the reasons the temporary relief of being drunk gets to be so precious is that getting drunk knocks one's conscience in the head. For a while the goddamned moralist within shuts up. That is wonderful for a little while, but when you sober up the moralist within works overtime. Then the payback is not just a hangover, it's a hangover in church. For this you need immediate relief, so you hit the bottle again. A vicious cycle.

Well-being is the antithesis of this cycle. Well-being starts with the dawning realization that you are being helplessly buffeted from non-awareness to sickness to temporary relief, and that despite your efforts to take care of yourself, you still end up in this vicious cycle.

When any client gets more than temporary relief from his or her learned system of culturally approved self-destructive behavior, then psychotherapy has worked. When people stop getting drunk or stoned or high incessantly and enjoy themselves more when they do those things occasionally, they have clearly started taking better care of themselves. There is no reason not to drink alcohol and smoke marijuana if you keep in good physical shape by working out, and if you don't have to have them to be happy.

We have all experienced well-being and have memories of times we felt whole and full and fine. Well-being has to be continually relearned and reexperienced through a redirection of attention away from the preconceptions of the mind and toward the experiences of excitement in the body. Once well-being as a continual process of noticing and rediscovery has been learned, the way a person spends time and what he or she does in his or her life changes noticeably.

Well-being is not taught in schools, by parents or by the church. Well-being is self-taught using guidance from people who don't know much more about it than you do.

Diet, exercise, and psychological healing programs can support people in learning to create wellness as a natural, on-going state of being. This approach is radically different from the typical moralism of the usual "try harder to do good" approach. In fact, such moralism is a primary source of injury and ill health among health freaks. Show me a moralist and I'll show you someone who doesn't know how to take care of him or herself. Only if people can learn to *un*do their dumb ways of trying-to-take-care-of-themselves-by-shoulding-all-over-themselves, can they heal more naturally, by letting up. If you're tired and sick take a break. Take it easy. Don't worry, be happy.

Some people will relearn how to take care of themselves and

some won't. Those of us in the helping professions who deal with stressed-out people know that not everyone will be successful in overcoming the ways of surviving that are killing them. We know that regardless of our best efforts to provide a place and a way of being that gives people the best chance to interrupt themselves on the road to slow suicide, many won't even slow their pace. Nevertheless, when intervention does work, this is how it is done: regardless of what or how the person is thinking, we interrupt the person's mind; then begin a conversation about personal power based on noticing rather than on thinking. When that conversation gets started, it will sometimes last a lifetime.

Most of the walking wounded can't tell down from up anymore. Because self-crippling people will continue to cripple themselves with any "self-improvement" program, we have to interrupt their mechanical replication of their own suffering before we can do anything other than waste time trying to teach them anything new. After that interruption, we can teach people the nuts and bolts of taking care of themselves. For this reason, telling the truth is central to all activities and programs of self-improvement.

The source of personal power is the ability to interrupt your own mind. And since having things to hide keeps you in your racing mind and keeps it racing, you have to reveal what you have hidden. The whole being that each of us is includes, but is not limited to, the mind. Nothing interrupts the mind like telling the truth. My judgment about whether therapy works is based on a few assumptions about what the job *is*, which I will now make explicit.

Psychotherapy and How it Works, When it Does

All illnesses, whether psychological or physical, are stress-related. Any complete job of psychotherapy must produce an observable and measurable change in physical tension, a decrease in the form of psychological misery the person first reports, and no new misery to take its place. Both the therapist and the client must perceive a decrease in the psychological misery complained about in the beginning. Equally important, other people who knew the client before therapy must notice that the person is more rested, more at ease, and less miserable, and not just screwed up in a new way.

Therapy doesn't always work. Sometimes when it does work, it works only for a while and then the person degenerates back to living out of more bullshit — this time about how well therapy worked — and loses whatever relearning occurred.

What happens when therapy works and keeps on working is that people want to learn about how to *stay* well. They become interested in living in the world by constantly renewing their leases on life rather than by being lost in their minds. They can do that best within the context of a sustaining community of other people in the same boat — people who have created wellness and are committed to maintaining wellness. Individuals who attain some new health and well-being need the support of such a community of friends, or the individual fades back into the cultural woodwork we are all dying from. It is from a position of support by a group of such people: friends, colleagues, and former clients of mine, that I write this book.

As I have worked with people under stress over the years, I have become more interested in life-management on the physical and immediate level, and less interested in the intricacies of deep psychological meaning. It is through this interest that I have discovered the practical value of telling the truth.

For about eight years I worked with and co-led groups with a psychiatrist who was without a doubt a genius, but whose life was incredibly screwed up, and remained so for as long as I knew him. He worked 12 hours a day, suffered from every bodily ailment known to man, went bankrupt every seven years, owed the IRS hundreds of thousands of dollars, couldn't keep a decent relationship going longer than a week, and was generally one of the poorer examples in this world of how to make life work. He treated his body like shit. He gave out advice to the tune of $300,000 a year, but his life didn't work. He didn't have time to take care of himself at the most basic level because he believed physical maintenance was a waste of time. He was great to talk to, and we had wonderful conversations about Joseph Campbell and the Sufis and personal and cultural mythology. But he was a pathetically miserable son-of-a-bitch and the best living proof I've seen that our minds' attempts to finally solve life's meaning are in no way related to the good life.

When we started out, he was my mentor. Later, we became colleagues. Eventually he was in therapy with me. The therapy was unsuccessful because he always knew the answer to everything, so there was no need to experiment with anything different. He didn't understand what anyone's grandmother could have told him: if you take care of your physical health, you do better. And if you don't, no matter how smart you are, you won't be very happy.

However, people don't take care of themselves out of knowing that they *should.* I had a friend whose doctor told him to lose fifteen pounds. When he went back for his next physical he had gained ten pounds instead, and his doctor kicked him out of the office saying, "If you aren't willing to take care of yourself, why in the hell should I?" That doctor is my doctor and has been for years, and I appreciate him for his anger and for his integrity. Still, despite this doctor's good intentions, my friend had to have a heart attack before he could learn to take care of himself. Fortunately, he didn't die and is in good shape today.

I too have kicked a lot of people out of my office, saying, "If you won't take care of yourself, to hell with you!" What bothers me more and more is that even though we are right, if we kicked everyone out who deserved being kicked out for not cooperating with us for his or her own good, there might not be anyone left, including ourselves.

Learning to take care of ourselves *creatively* rather than *resentfully* is a big step in growing up. When we take such good care of ourselves that we have all we need, the overflow to generosity with others is possible. Prior to that, nurturing relationships between or among adults are not possible. Prior to that, all gifts are bribes — everything has a string attached because you need something from the person you are giving the supposedly free gift to.

Most people won't give up on trying to force others to take care of them because they won't forgive their early caretakers for not having done a perfect job. Forgiveness is critical to physical and psychological health. When people can spend more time in the pleasant and lighter experiential continuum than in the miserable semi-darkness of the mind, they are healthier. The primary, fundamental, essential, baseline, critical, lowest-level minimum requirement for happiness, without which there is no other hope, is a *willingness to take care of oneself.* The trouble is, people are generally willing to take care of almost anyone or anything else BUT themselves. They will take care of a car, house, child, job, pet, boss, deadline, spouse, stranger, or any number of people and things on an endless list before they take care of themselves. Repeated observation of this phenomenon has led me to the conclusion that there is a particular *un*learning required for human growth to continue beyond adolescence, and most people don't unlearn it. What must be unlearned is the habit of being lost in value judgments that override experience. My teen-aged nephew would rather look cool, while freezing to death waiting for the school bus, than wear a warm jacket that is not as "in" as the shirt he is wearing. Most people don't grow beyond such adolescent tricks with or without therapy. Most therapists are still adolescents themselves and therefore don't know what the job is.

Many people are trapped at a certain stage of development, cut off from an essential feedback system that would naturally allow them to take care of themselves. The feedback system is built into all of us, but we have dissociated ourselves from it. The system requires that we pay attention to excitement in the body, rather than concepts in the mind. We all have the capacity to be aware of various forms of excitement in our bodies, but we don't pay much attention to that because we are too busy thinking and "shoulding" on ourselves.

For many of us, the older we get, the worse we are at taking care of ourselves. This is partly because we have learned too much about what we *should* do, and it blocks our ability to live based on what we *notice*. Rather than attending to what we know we *should* do, we can pay attention to our bodies — our ongoing bio-feedback system — and operate according to that, rather than our memories of what we learned before.

Getting Unstuck

If you don't take good care of yourself, find a therapist. Find a good one (who agrees with what I have just said). One clue to assist you in finding a therapist or a group to support you in staying whole and healthy is this: just talking is not enough. Talking therapies alone are obsolete and on the way out. Any therapist that conspires with your mind to try to help you think your way out of unhealth is not going to help you. I will give some ex-amples of "more than just talking" therapy in this chapter.

I combine techniques that many other professionals use separately, and I string them together in such a way that the combination works more powerfully than any of the separate treatments alone. I will outline a typical first ten sessions or so to illustrate.

When I begin seeing a new client, I listen and observe, get a feel for the person, and get a list of his or her complaints. Usually there is something pressing, some depth of depression or anxiety that has been insoluble longer than people can tolerate, so they break down and try therapy. Usually they are tired, so I work with them fairly early on to restore their bodies and help them recover from fatigue. I sometimes use polarity therapy — a pressure-point technique similar to reflexology and acupuncture. I pull their toes and put pressure on certain spots above connective tissue to teach their bodies directly how to relax. Many people don't consider lying on the floor getting their feet squeezed to be psychotherapy, so I get to violate their expectations right away. I don't know if the theories about energy behind polarity therapy or acupressure are correct or not, but I do know from doing polarity therapy for years that it works to relax people whether they want to relax or not. It hurts a little bit. It may work just because I teach people to relax unnecessary tension in the rest of their body in order to decrease pain in the spot where I'm pushing. It may be that just the tensing and relaxing that naturally occurs when someone is hurting your toes results in an overall relaxation. It may be that people learn that an appropriate way to deal with physical pain is to be fully willing to experience the pain where it hurts, and, instead of tensing up the rest of their body in response to the pain, to relax the rest of their body and take what they get — and they generalize that to the psychological domain. Whatever the cause, people are more relaxed after I've worked on them for thirty minutes than they were before. They feel better and can sleep and get rested that very night. They have also learned something about how *resistance* causes pain to persist and *surrender* causes pain to decrease.

Any problems I notice in the dynamic of holding on and letting go in the body usually show up as well when they describe their relationships to people, money, and time. This fact becomes evident in conversation, when I continue the process. This period of hearing their complaints and teaching them to start work on *themselves* rather than *on those complained about* lasts two or three sessions. This sometimes takes longer if they get pissed off or shocked that their "way of being" about their complaints, rather than what's being complained about, is the source of the problem and the focus of therapy.

Also in this first phase, I often ask clients to allow me to hypnotize them. Right after the polarity therapy work is a good time for this, because they are already deeply relaxed. While they are in a trance state, I teach them self-hypnosis and suggest that they will get very good at it through regular practice at home. As a part of the hypnotic induction I explain to them very thoroughly some of the functions of the involuntary nervous system and the power of the unconscious mind in self-healing. I remind them again of another method of control they have used before but forgotten, the method of control through surrender. I teach them to relax and let the involuntary nervous system run things without interference, because it does the most important work anyway. They get the message that they can start taking care of themselves based on what they *notice* about themselves when they relax and pay attention. If they are tired, as many of them are, they can rest. If they are hungry they can eat. If they are thirsty, they can drink. If they feel shitty, they can do things to feel better. (This is what Wilhelm Reich called organismic self-regulation.) When I just tell people this, most of them will agree in theory and still not do it. If I teach them self-hypnosis and have them "notice their noticing," sometimes, from practicing noticing, the lesson actually soaks in.

Over about a six-week period, we talk some more about their troubles. I might do another session of polarity therapy on them and they continue to practice self-hypnosis. I also give them body awareness exercises. Sometimes I teach them yoga exercises, do bio-feedback, or use other physical manipulation or instructional techniques. I sometimes use cerebral electro-stimulation or "sleep machine" treatments, in which a person uses stethoscope-style electrodes powered by nine-volt batteries to induce a low current to the brain to bring about more restful sleep. (The "Cerebral Electro-Stimulation" machine is classified as a research tool by the Food and Drug Administration. The research on sleep machines has been going on for 40 years, and it works to induce a normal sleep pattern so people can get rested, but nobody knows why yet.)

I don't particularly care why things work. If something works most of the time with people, I use it. Half the things I do may seem to be pure hocus-pocus, but they often work.

Some years ago, I saw a young man of 23 whose bowels moved only once every three days. He had terrible hemorrhoids, and couldn't ejaculate when he had sex. He could ejaculate sometimes when he masturbated, but that was painful. There was a tightness throughout the lower half of his body. I sent him to a proctologist to find out what to do for his hemorrhoids. The proctologist told him he should have them operated on and he would have to go into the hospital for the operation because his case was too severe to be treated on an in-and-out basis. He agreed to go into the hospital, but he put it off, as he had done before. I was working with him in therapy and did what I described above: polarity therapy, hypnosis, self-hypnosis, and some extra Gestalt therapy work on anger. By the fourth one-hour long sleep machine and deep relaxation treatment, he ejaculated during sexual intercourse with his girlfriend. Although he had experienced intercourse many times, this was the first time in his life he had ever had an orgasm during intercourse. He started having bowel movements every day without any trouble. The hemorrhoids went away except for the sacs. He went back to the doctor who now said he didn't have to have an operation but could have the sacs cut off if he wanted. That was eleven years ago, and the man still ejaculates without pain, and although he does occasionally have problems with hemorrhoids, they are nothing like what they were before.

Along with these physical treatments, he had some honest conversations with his girlfriend. He re-established contact with his mother. He revealed some of his fear and anger. These things, these reversals of his earlier "tight-assed" control of his feelings and secrets, allowed him to keep the "temporary" benefits of polarity therapy, sleep-machine treatments, bioenergetics, biofeedback, and self-hypnosis.

I have assisted people to cure themselves of asthma, lower-back pain, skin rashes, insomnia, obesity, alcohol, nicotine and drug addictions, and other bodily ailments. I have also failed to help a few. But generally, I can turn people on to the power of taking charge of their own experience in their bodies to heal themselves of bodily ills. We eventually find something that works. It also turns out that the same thing works to straighten out relationships. When we become willing to take full responsibility for taking care of our own selves in the world, our relationships start working better, as do our bodies. Most of us, unfortunately, want to make someone else take care of us instead. We can all still remember — consciously or not — how nice it was when we were small enough that someone else had to do the worrying and the work. Although it is a complete waste of time to work your ass off trying to rearrange the world into that previous model that worked a long time ago, most of us never get that message.

So the first phase of therapy is body therapy, and beginning instruction in self-maintenance through noticing and physical discipline. The physical techniques like Yoga, polarity therapy, and self-hypnosis, have only temporary effects, but people can keep the benefits of these crisis-oriented therapeutic techniques if they take over the task of taking care of themselves physically on a regular basis and learn to rest and relax and nurture themselves.

Next, the person enters into an agreement with me to work out and get in good physical shape, and I assist them with support for a kind of spring training. After those beginning weeks, we make some agreements about exercise, nutrition, drugs and alcohol, and other matters of physical health, and we begin psychotherapy the way other people think of it.

The hardest part of what we do is the characterological part — the therapy to change the way the person runs him- or herself. The ways we all learned to get satisfaction that worked at eight years of age become increasingly less appropriate as we grow older, but the unconscious mind doesn't get the message. Insights gained in childhood become principles of control for living the "right life" as an adult. But people have to get over childhood in order to grow up. Growing up is not just a continual accumulation of new learning: you have to ditch some of what you learned before. One particularly effective way to do this is to tell the truth about all your attempts to manipulate others to get what you want. Until you can laugh about this, you aren't free from being manipulated by your own manipulations. It is only through telling the truth about all these hidden agendas for getting what you want that the real work of growing begins.

So at this third phase of therapy, some of the work is ferreting out current manipulations or attempts at manipulation, and various forms of emotional blackmail learned earlier in life, and confessing them to the historical and the current victims. Since pictures of how one is supposed to be taken care of, and models for getting what one wants by conning others, become entrenched in the mind as how things *should* be, much of this work involves disappointment, anger, and sadness. Coaching during this phase of therapy involves everything I've written about in this book so far.

Therapy consists primarily of teaching people how to recontact the experience that exists below their moralism, or below *ideas* about life is and how it should be. The *experiencer* normally blocked by moralistic resolve will then gradually come to the foreground, and the moralism, while remaining intact, will recede to the background. One's life changes, of course, after such a transformation, but the point is not the change. The circumstantial changes are almost incidental; the point is the shift of figure and ground. The figure in the foreground, the mind-bound, harried, "shouldistic" warrior, moves to the background — still alive and

[211]

well and whole, but no longer leading — and the heretofore background figure, the quiet animal who walks and laughs, taking what's so in nature, comes to the foreground — even in the city, and even at work. Such a shift is a matter of grace and strikes only those in good-feeling shape who are ready to receive it. Being a good therapist is knowing this and helping the odds along.

People can be turned on to their own power and goodness enough that they don't need tightly held *principles* to hold themselves together anymore. It is here that visions of a more heroic life arise. They arise from the same depths that the self-crippling principles of control came from. They arise this time, however, at the behest of a person who *feels* like creating and affirming his or her life, rather than a person who feels sick and bad and powerless. It is precisely at this point, the most visceral and basic point of physical experience, that the power of personal responsibility for well-being emerges. People discover how to take care of themselves when they come back in contact with their experience. No one has time to *discover* anything when they are constantly being swamped by orders from central casting. These orders, given in a shrill internal tone of voice, were built in with feelings of shame at eight years of age or earlier. When we are not unthinkingly obeying that voice, we handle our daily, physical, basic, on-going existence with energy left over and worry decreased, and we are able to get in touch with our power as creators. Psychological well-being comes out of the re-discovery that you are the Creator. Most of our education is to prevent such a thing from happening.

A lot of what I'm saying is familiar to a lot of people, with the possible exception of most practicing psychologists and psychiatrists. "Talking-only" psychotherapy by itself is an anachronism. The traditional Freudian psychoanalytical approach has already bitten the dust except as a *post hoc* creative mythology for those already cured, or not interested in being cured, of anxiety or depression. On the way in are people who take care of themselves, now and then using a doctor or therapist who knows something about stress and understands transformation. People are learning to give up looking for an authority to take care of their hurt and make it all better, and instead are looking for a fellow human with modern technology at hand and a vision of a better way to live. These are my kind of people. People like this are creators who use me creatively, and when they are like this they don't *need* me anymore — they *use* me to their best advantage.

What I think we learn together, over and over, is something about giving up. We give up wishing. We abandon all hope. Life becomes a game for the sake of the game alone. The act of wishing is itself transformed. Nietzsche said, "A man's maturity consists in having found again the seriousness one had as a child at play."[1] That serious play, that paying attention first and then thinking-directed-by-attention, that utter dedication to *being with* whatever you are doing, is a way of being we have known since the light first came on in the womb. We keep trying to get a grasp on this ungraspable being by remembering what it did and predicting what it will do. That doesn't work. What fools us into being neurotic is the desire to hold on to some experiences and to avoid others. Experience changes constantly, so we move to fantasies and worries which also change — but at a slower rate. This gives us a sense of control. Most of us will trade anything we have for a good false sense of control.

If we can surrender the false sense of control provided by protective beliefs and fantasies of who we are and how we *should* be, we can learn to use the mind-machine we originally developed as a defense against the nuns and teachers and other cops. Now, centered in our experience, we can use our minds as instruments for creating. When a person learns to use his or her own mind for creating, rather than being used by that mind, the job of psychotherapy is over. ⌐

PART

IV

Things Learned from the
War between Being & Mind

ABOUT CHANGE

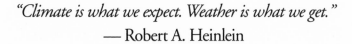

"Climate is what we expect. Weather is what we get."
— Robert A. Heinlein

THIS CHAPTER describes where power comes from. Power resides in persons, not in techniques.

In John Steinbeck's *The Grapes of Wrath*[1], Tom Joad and his brother Al, in the middle of their trek from Oklahoma to California with the whole family and all their worldly goods, had to go to a junkyard to get a part needed to overhaul the engine on their car. They had borrowed a truck from some people in the same shape they were.

> The truck drove to the service station belt, and there on the right-hand side of the road was a wrecking yard — an acre lot surrounded by a high barbed-wire fence, a corrugated iron shed in front with used tires piled up by the doors, and price-marked. Behind the shed there was a little shack built of scrap, scrap lumber and pieces of tin. The windows were windshields built into the walls. In the greasy lot the wrecks lay, cars with twisted,

stove-in noses, wounded cars lying on their sides with the wheels gone. Engines rusting on the ground and against the shed. A great pile of junk; fenders and truck sides, wheels and axles; over the whole lot a spirit of decay, of mold and rust; twisted iron, half-gutted engines, a mass of derelicts.

Al drove the truck up on the oily ground in front of the shed. Tom got out and looked into the dark doorway. "Don't see nobody," he said, and he called, "Anybody here? Jesus I hope they got a '25 Dodge."

Behind the shed a door banged. A specter of a man came through the dark shed. Thin, dirty, oily skin tight against stringy muscles. One eye was gone, and the raw, uncovered socket squirmed with eye muscles when his good eye moved. His jeans and shirt were thick and shiny with old grease, and his hands cracked and lined and cut. His heavy, pouting underlip hung out sullenly.

Tom asked, "You the boss?"

The one eye glared. "I work for the boss," he said sullenly. "Whatcha want?"

"Got a wrecked '25 Dodge? We need a con-rod."

"I don't know. If the boss was here he could tell ya — but he ain't here. He's went home."

"Can we look and see?"

The man wiped his nose into the palm of his hand and wiped his hand on his trousers. "You from hereabouts?"

"Come from east — goin' west."

"Look aroun' then. Burn the goddamn place down, for all I care."

"Looks like you don't love your boss none."

The man shambled close, his one eye flaring. "I hate 'im," he said softly. "I hate the son-of-a-bitch! Gone home now. Gone home to his house." The words fell stumbling out. "He got a way — he got a way a-pickin' a fella an' a-tearin' a fella. He — the son-of-a-bitch. Got a girl nineteen, purty. Says to me, 'How'd you like to marry her?' Says that right to me. An' tonight says, 'They's a dance; how'd ya like ta go?' Me, he says it to me!" Tears formed in his eye and dripped from the corner of the red eye socket. "Some day, by God — some day I'm gonna have a pipe wrench in my pocket. When he says them things he looks at my eye. An' I'm gonna, I'm gonna jus' take his head right down off his neck with that wrench, little piece at a time." He panted with his fury. "Little piece at a time, right down off'n his neck."

The sun disappeared behind the mountains. Al looked into the lot at the wrecked cars. "Over there, look, Tom! That there looks like a '25 or '26."

Tom turned to the one-eyed man. "Mind if we look?"

"Hell no! Take any Goddamned thing you want," the one-eyed man said. "I'll get you a box a tools." He shuffled off among the rusty cars and in a moment he came back with a tin box of tools. Tom dug out a socket wrench and handed it to Al.

"You take her off. Don' lose no shims an' don' let the bolts get away, an' keep track a the cotter-pins. Hurry up. The light's gettin' dim."

Al crawled under the car. "We oughta get us a set a socket wrenches," he called. "Can't get in no place with a monkey wrench."

"Yell out if you want a hand," Tom said.

The one-eyed man stood helplessly by. "I'll help ya if ya want," he said.

"Know what that son-of-a-bitch done? He come by an' he got on white pants. An' he says, 'Come on, le's go out to my yacht.' By God, I'll whang him some day!" He breathed heavily, "I ain't been out with a woman sence I los' my eye. An' he says stuff like that." And big tears cut channels in the dirt beside his nose.

Tom said impatiently, "Whyn't you roll on? Got no guards to keep ya here."

"Yeah, that's easy to say. Ain't so easy to get a job — not for a one-eye' man."

Tom turned on him. "Now look-a-here, fella. You got that eye wide open. An' ya dirty, ya stink. Ya' jus' askin' for it. Ya like it. Let's ya feel sorry for yaself. 'Course ya can't get no woman with that empty eye flappin' aroun'. Put somepin over it an' wash ya face. You ain't hittin' nobody with no pipe wrench."

"I tell ya, a one-eye' fella got a hard row," the man said. "Can't see stuff the way other fellas can. Can't see how far off a thing is. Ever'thing's jus' flat."

Tom said, "Ya full a crap. Why, I knowed a one-legged whore one time. Think she was takin' two-bits in a alley? No, by God! She's gettin' half a dollar extra. She says, 'How many one-legged women you slep' with? None!' she says. 'O.K.,' she says, 'You got somepin pretty special here, an' it's gonna cos' ya half a buck extry.' An' by God, she was gettin' 'em, too, an' the fellas comin' out thinkin' they're pretty lucky. She says she's good luck. An' I knowed a hump-back in — in a place I was. Make his whole livin' lettin' folks rub his hump for luck. Jesus Christ, an' all you got is one eye gone."

The man said stumblingly, "Well, Jesus, ya see somebody edge away from ya, and it gets into ya."

"Cover it up then, goddamn it. Ya stickin' it out like a cow's ass. Ya like to feel sorry for yaself. There ain't nothin' the matter with you. Buy yaself some white pants. Ya gettin' drunk and cryin' in ya bed, I bet. Need any help, Al?"

The one-eyed man said softly, "Think — somebody'd like — me?"

"Why, sure," said Tom. "Tell 'em ya dong's growed sence you los' your eye."

"Where at you fellas goin'?"

"California. Whole family. Gonna get work out there."

"Well, ya think a fella like me could get work? Black patch on my eye?"

"Why not? You ain't no cripple."

"Well — could I catch a ride with you fellas?"

"Christ, no. We're so goddamn full now we can't move. You get out some other way. Fix up one a these here wrecks an' go out by yaself."

"Maybe I will, by God," said the one-eyed man."

What Tom said to the one-eyed man was what I call a great therapeutic intervention. But even radical interventions by the best of therapists are powerless unless there is a commitment by a whole and undivided being to change. All of the information in the world is of no value, and all research is irrelevant, until placed in the context of the power of intention.

We all display a kind of inconsistency among our beliefs, our wishes, and our actions in our own lives, although it may be easier to recognize in the lives of others. We have all listened to an argument play itself out between two (or more) voices within our own minds — one preaching about what we should do, and the other helplessly apologizing and explaining about how we would if we could but we can't. We all share an awareness, if we are honest, that on some fundamental level, the apparent struggle among our beliefs, actions, and desires is a false one. More often than not, the "struggle" has emerged after a choice has already been made, though perhaps unconsciously. The "struggle" manifests itself mostly as effort: "trying" to decide; "trying" to be good; "trying" to keep our word. The false struggle is invented by our minds as a distraction, to "draw fire" — to draw the fire of our attention and keep us from seeing that we have already chosen.

nto the truck. It was deep dark. Al
started the motor and turned on the lights. "So long,"
Tom called. "See ya maybe in California." They turned
across the highway and started back.

The one-eyed man watched them go, and then he
went through the iron shed to his shack behind. It was
dark inside. He felt his way to the mattress on the floor,
and he stretched out and cried in his bed, and the cars
whizzing by on the highway only strengthened the walls
of his loneliness.

When people view themselves as conglomerations of opposing
forces, each force straining in a different direction with each
particular component striving to wrest control from the others
and dominate the future, the result is a sense of helplessness.
Impotent fury is weakness. Effort is the opposite of power. That
aspect of our experience that longs for happiness and righteousness never quite succeeds in gaining control over the other forces,
which we view as alien and unwanted "baggage" — the unfortu-
nate accidents of our character that somehow overpower our
inner longings and cover up our true selves. We imagine that
stronger or luckier people have succeeded in their battle for
self-control, and that this is the source of their power. This belief
that others have succeeded where we have failed becomes just
another element in our battle against ourselves: our longing to be
that which we are not.

The conditions we produce in our lives, the actions we repeat against our will, the circumstances that make us suffer — somehow we have perpetuated them, despite our professed beliefs and our efforts to change.

The source of our power to produce the results we want does not lie in our beliefs, our hopes, or our time-consuming struggle to change. The person who says he wants to lose weight, but says he just can't give up midnight snacks, may believe he is in a struggle between "being good" and "giving in" to his cravings, but in fact he has already chosen to keep snacking. The "struggle" that he describes serves to hide this fact.

By focusing our attention on our apparent struggle to change — the reasons and explanations and excuses that we generate instead of results — we engage in a conspiracy to pretend that we are each an accidental grouping of disharmonious parts working against each other. Why "parts"? When you say, "I want to look for a new job, but I can't seem to get started," who is it that "wants to" and who is it that "can't"? It is as though there were two of you and one — the one who "can't" — had more power than the other. You pretend that the "real" you is the one that "wants to." We pretend that we are not whole. The "I" who wants to get up early every morning and exercise, for instance, seems to be a different individual from the "I" who decides to sleep in. The "I" who longs for a successful, supportive marriage is not the "I" who backs down from making a commitment whenever a relationship gets too serious. Instead of examining more closely the actual way in which we operate, which consists of "trying" to get what we want and then sabotaging our own efforts, we assume our error is in not trying hard enough, and redouble both our efforts and our resistance. We always manage to stay one step ahead of ourselves, so that we never quite reach our goals. By focusing on the struggle instead of on the results, we avoid having to admit that the one who wants to change and the one who resists change are one and the same, that we are whole, and that we really *do* get what we want — which is struggle, rather than results. But until I can experience my own resistance as "me" just as I experience my desire to change as "me," I am doomed to be locked in the hopeless struggle for control. Tom was absolutely right about the one-eyed man: "Ya jus' askin' for it. Ya like it. Lets ya feel sorry for yaself."

Instead of amalgamations of parts having contradictory and uncontrollable purposes, suppose we consider ourselves to be already what we long to be: functional, integrated wholes who produce the results we choose, effortlessly, with our entire beings. Suppose we all, already, are that. All the apparent contradictions and dichotomies — the fat person struggling to be thin, the sinner trying to be good, the workaholic longing for time with his family — are actually smokescreens, false struggles enacted by our own minds to hide from others or ourselves our true intent. Our true intent is to do just what we do.

As complete, integrated human beings, we direct our lives with purpose, with effortless control, and with unchecked power. This is scary. The contradictions between our principles and our behavior are only superficial, only invented for the sake of appearance and to avoid acknowledging our terrifying power to make things happen. Our unwillingness to explore the possibility that what we have is what we want — that our lives function,

that we are comfortable and fear change in most areas of our lives
— prevents us from producing change in other areas. Our energy
is totally invested in maintaining our lives the way they are, and
the phony struggle for change only conceals the ways in which
the status quo serves us. Our apparent battle for change is a
tempest in a teapot. As long as I identify my "self" only as that
desire to change and not also as a presently more powerful desire
to remain the same, I will remain stuck. In a sense, I can change,
finally, only by giving up *trying* to change.

In order for things to get better, they must first get worse. In
order to get out of debt, we have to acknowledge how it serves us
to be in debt. In order to lose weight, we have to be in touch
with, and confront, how we also want to stay fat. We have to stop
paying attention to our struggle and turn our awareness to the
ways in which these circumstances we claim we want to change
serve us — the payoffs. Only after experiencing ourselves the
way we are, dropping our phony struggle to change, and telling
the truth about all of it, can we create the lives we have been
saying we want.

This examination of our subconscious desire to avoid change,
and of what lies beneath the phony struggle, can get us "unstuck."
It also leads to a deeper place, a scarier place, than that of mere
struggle to change. Struggling to change is what you do to hide
from something worse. Struggling to change is a way to avoid
facing the abyss, and if the abyss *could* be avoided, it would be a
good idea.

The abysmal truth is that everything comes to nothing. No
change matters. Whatever you don't have is only important to

you because you don't have it. Something you want is very important to you until you get it, and then it's nothing after a while. This movement from anticipation to accomplishment to disillusionment is inevitable. All change is futile. The alternative kind of life — conservative, preserving beliefs, avoiding change, a kind of stagnation within the protected bounds of first-learned concepts — is an equally futile way to live. Both ways to live are merely playing tiddlywinks between predoom and postdoom. Willingness to face the abyss of meaninglessness is the power required to accomplish change. Whatever your main struggle is, it is insignificant in the face of your death; it is petty and unimportant and has no meaning at all. It is a tale told by an idiot, full of sound and fury, signifying nothing.

Intention

When we are locked in a losing battle for self-control, our attempts to change are marked by effort and by "trying." When we are whole, the power of our intention becomes available to us. What is being whole? What do I mean by "intention"?

Being whole means including everything. Being whole includes the experience of eternal time after the light came on in the womb, the experiences of differentiation and individuation that come with growing up, the current electrical current we are this moment, all our imaginings, and facing death. Being this wholeness allows for intention to be possible.

Like obscenity, intention is hard to define, but easy to recognize. Each of us has had experiences of effortless change or accomplishment — results that we produced so effortlessly, and often against such odds, that it seemed almost as though they were done through us instead of by us. It's not that they weren't difficult or challenging. It's that we were somehow free to confront the tasks, to throw the full force of our minds and bodies into them, rather than somehow, inexplicably, held back from within. Intention that calmly comes from wholeness is like that. People who have had such an experience often remark, "I don't really know how I did it. I just did it. I guess I was just ready." They didn't experience having control over themselves in quite the way that we imagine "will power" or "self-control" to work; yet there was never a question about their commitment to continue. It's as though the strength of their intention actually eliminated the need for self-control because they were no longer fighting themselves. It would have required more effort to stop than to continue. Once some decision was made in the quiet, private sanctuary of the self, by the whole person, and once the world was informed of that decision, bringing about the certain outcome was only a matter of time.

In sports, this magic fascinates us by the millions as observers and by the hundreds of thousands as participants. The most incredible performances, that take everything a person has, have the grace of effortless nonchalance. We all have areas of our lives in which we work in this effortless, powerfully creative way, and other areas in which we struggle impotently without results. Those whose creative power has been unavailable to them in an area they want to change can rediscover this power of intention when they seriously take responsibility for creating their whole lives right now, including their phony smokescreen struggle.

Responsibility

Responsibility means that whatever you are doing, you are willing to experience yourself as the cause. You are the source of your troubles as well as of your successes. Wherever you are on the way to reaching your goals — whether you are cruising along, pulled over to the side of the road, or feel like you're going backwards — the willingness to experience yourself as responsible is the crucial element of success. As long as you are blaming, explaining, apologizing, trying, resolving to be good, hoping or feeling guilty, you are not being responsible. *Trying* to experience yourself as responsible won't work. What you *can* do is declare yourself responsible, and then see what happens. It *is* possible to interrupt the powerless games we play to avoid being responsible. When we begin to interrupt those games, we can move on.

One of these games is called, "Okay, okay, I'm guilty." This game is to make it look like you have taken responsibility for yourself when you haven't. Admitting you are guilty is a great way to avoid being responsible. There is a big difference between admitting you are guilty of failure, or "copping a plea," and really owning your power as the creator of your life. Whether you *feel* guilty or not is irrelevant. Admitting you are wrong or were wrong is only a prelude to taking responsibility for your life. It is not enough. You have to make a commitment after you interrupt this game. After you acknowledge that you've been fooling yourself by trying hard, you have to make a public declaration of what you will now be responsible for creating. Stick your neck out. Put your ass on the line. Tell everybody what you are about, and by when you will get results, and ask them to help.

We all know that commitment is essential to creation. What has been unclear in our culture is what to do when you're not committed to anything but struggle. When we feel powerless to keep our word, eventually we stop giving it. Your wholeness — the experience of yourself the way you are — must precede commitment, because to be anything less than your whole self is to be trapped in the morass of beliefs you have about who you are based on your case history. Commitment must be based on the awareness of what *is*, and on the willingness to be responsible for ourselves the way we are. That means if we are imperfect beings who make mistakes, break our word, get angry, and are selfish, greedy, petty, and unfair, we must make our commitment as those imperfect beings. We spend our lives waiting to get better so that we can accept ourselves. We refuse to enjoy life, refuse to accept that we are loved and forgiven, and refuse to tell the truth about who we are because we never quite meet our *own* standards. Perfectionists are people who would rather be the worst than be the second-best. Everyone who ever successfully made a change that worked and served as a platform for the next, did this first: they finally accepted themselves the way they were. They gave up the struggle to get better. Then, finally, they were free to change.

The source of your historical being and the source of your present being is like a generator that has been constant since it started. Getting back to your source is the first technique for change. When you pay attention to the being you are, you withdraw attention from the dilemmas of your mind.

This is at the heart of Buddhism, Yoga, Vedantic Philosophy, Christian salvation, and other forms and practices of enlightenment. When a Zen Buddhist sits and looks at a wall for fourteen hours a day for seven days in a row, he does it to be able to sit and look at a wall. To be able to sit and look at a wall and *just* sit and look at a wall is enlightenment. To sit and look at your life story like you would sit and look at a wall is to recontact your source in the same way.

Your heartbeat started about eight weeks after the egg that became you got fertilized. You tuned in to life by growing into attunement. That is who you are. To get back in touch with who you are when you have been lost in your mind is to get back to your source.

This is hard to do. You have to die to live. Your "pretend" self, that doesn't include your imperfection, has to die. Then, you again become a whole being. You then have the power you have always had, only now you can use it consciously. This is the good life. It requires that you sacrifice the pleasure of crying yourself to sleep on a greasy mattress.

THE TRUTH CHANGES

*"Thinking that the self must remain constant for life to
have meaning is like falling hopelessly in love with an inch."*
— Alan Watts

AT THE ONE HUNDREDTH ANNIVERSARY of Psychotherapy
conference in Phoenix, in December of 1985, the psychiatrist
R.D. Laing demonstrated his therapeutic method in a public
conversation with a homeless woman who had come into a shelter off the streets the night before. Laing and the woman were in
an enclosed room, and she knew that a video camera was "watching"
them, and that the video was being projected to a couple of
thousand people in an audience nearby.

When she started talking, she made a number of abstract
theological statements about the nature of the universe. Laing
simply engaged her in conversation and said what he had sometimes thought about the same subjects. They had a fairly pleasant
conversation in which he listened to her and she listened to him.
At the end of the conversation he said, "I have to go out to the
audience now and talk to the people about our conversation,"
and she said, "Well, I'll go with you." So she came out and sat

next to Laing on the panel of experts answering questions from the floor.

As far as Laing was concerned, his interaction with the woman spoke for itself. That was an example of what therapy is: engaging another person, getting who she is, letting her be and letting her "get" that she has been "gotten," and, in turn, letting her get who the therapist is, how he is and what he believes.

A number of psychiatrists and social workers and psychologists in the audience insisted on knowing what, of therapeutic value, had happened in the interaction: "What did you do? What was the result? What was the effect?" How did Laing know he had done anything? Had it been worth doing? Was it going to help her to change?

In response, Laing spoke mostly of the self-sufficiency of the interaction, asserting that contact between he and the woman had been complete. As human beings, they had connected, and, that was the point. Laing even angrily directed one persistent questioner to sit down and let someone else ask a question because he was tired of putting up with loaded questions — questions that seemed to insist that the point of therapy had to be some goal beyond the experience of contact. From Laing's point of view, the questioner could see therapy only as the therapist manipulating the client into a different way of behaving. Laing's goal, as he demonstrated, was simply to be present with a person and let them work out a way of being with you. Supporting her in working out her way of being in the world, he had made a connection with her, such that when he came out to discuss their conversation with the audience, she came along to help and see what else there was to be learned.

Many of the therapists there could not understand the conversation to be sufficient as therapy because they looked only for evidence of change according to a certain conceptual framework: an "improved" patient would reform her behavior, change her speech, say certain things, etc. Bondage to this conceptual framework prevented some members of the audience from seeing other kinds of changes, such as changes in willingness, way of being, or relaxation and openness, which were clearly evident in the woman's behavior after working with Laing.

The point is that, regardless of therapists' judgments, people have already worked out, and will continue to work out, their ways of being in the world. But their contact with the world changes when they are contacted. The truth changes for them through being heard. One creator of the world is in conversation with another.

I agree with Laing and I share his objective, but with one additional goal: I'm interested in a conversation *about* our conversation that includes the possibility of living as a creator *consciously*. When I engage in a conversation in which I create a connection with another person through listening, I want to speak to the creator of that conversation. I want to talk with the creator being, and I want to talk about creation. People interested in creation notice that *what* they notice changes. A change in noticing leads to escape from the self-fulfilling prophecy of the previous self-and world-view, and leads into a new world, and this occurs over and over again.

Surviving vs. Being Alive

We all have trouble staying alive as opposed to just surviving. Usually, unless something catastrophic occurs, we stay in a conceptual world, and we have trouble really perceiving. We don't perceive because we choose the comfort and security of what we already "know" over the ambiguity of experience.

William Coles, a teacher of creative writing, says of his students: "Students have trouble writing, after all, because they have trouble reading; they have trouble reading because they don't hear; and they don't hear because they don't take time to listen. The same difficulty, by the way, is at the root of the trouble they have at being engineers or biologists or English majors or citizens or parents or sons or husbands."[1]

To rephrase Cole's text: People have trouble living because they have trouble thinking; they have trouble thinking because they don't perceive with their senses; and they don't perceive with their senses because they don't interrupt their minds' constant reshuffling of worn-out but familiar concepts. The same difficulty is at the root of their difficulty in being husbands, wives, fathers, sons, daughters, friends, and lovers. To *perceive* and conceive anew, rather than *reconceive*, is the whole challenge. One has to re-open oneself beyond preconception over and over again. It feels like dying. Coming alive always feels like dying, because you are giving up your previous conceptual orientation — your previous personality — for a new and uncertain beginning. To quote e.e. cummings again: "Most people fancy a guaranteed birth-proof safety suit of non-destructible selflessness. If most people were to be born twice they'd improbably call it dying."[2]

You and I think we have learned from experience, and that it is important to remember those lessons. We do learn from experience, but those lessons are not as helpful as we think. What we most frequently do is make bad recordings of distortions of experience and get off on feeling smug about them. These recordings become the jail of the mind. This memory jail needs to be inhibited rather than inhabited.

In promoting inhibition of domination by the mind, I am not talking about something new in history, just something relatively new to western history. Yoga, which means yoke — that which connects together intellect and spirit, or being and mind — is primarily concerned with exactly the topic we are now considering. In the millennia-old philosophy and practice of yoga, as summarized in the Yoga Sutras of Patanjali, countering the mind's distortions is given the highest priority.

In Sanskrit, there is a form of embodying all there is to be known about any area of study into 100 *sutras*, or verses. These are short phrases, limited to about a two-line statement, organized in a specific form. The first sutra says what these sutras are all about. For example if we were to put the whole body of knowledge we call physics into one hundred statements, the first statement would be, "These are the sutras of Physics." Then we would have 99 statements left to cover all of physics. The second sutra is designated as the most comprehensive overview of the whole of the work and practices of the area under consideration. In our example, we would be expected, in the second sutra, to say in one statement what all of physics is about. Patanjali, after Yoga had been around for a few thousand years, wrote the Yoga

Sutras. By the time he wrote the Yoga Sutras, many different methods for the practice of Yoga had been developed: Karma Yoga, Bakti Yoga, Tantric Yoga, Kundalini Yoga, Hatha Yoga and so on. These yogas of service, love, sex, work, physical health, and the philosophy of yoga had all undergone literally thousands of years of development. The second sutra of the Yoga Sutras, the one that most comprehensively covers its subject, says, "The objective of all Yoga is to bring about *an inhibition of the modifications of the mind.*"[3] [emphasis mine].

The modifications of the mind are memories, principles, conclusions, morals, and beliefs. Telling the truth is the particular "yogic" practice necessary *in our time* to inhibit them.

Growing Beyond the Developmental Stage of Learning How to Lie

It is okay that we all learned to lie. Learning how to lie and to withhold is a necessary developmental stage, crucial to getting on in life and getting around in the world. Cognitive and personality development cannot occur without developing essential lying skills. We learn to condense experience, and we then all, individually, experience the problem of reductionism. Lying is a result of re-ductionism — the condensation of memory and the categori-zation of experience we naturally learn while growing up. When we start thinking with categories, we exclude a lot of experience; yet, we need the efficiency of thinking with categories.

As we learn categories for the sake of efficiency, we learn at the same time to avoid experience. A one-year-old child sits in the yard and looks up at an airplane flying over. The child listens to the plane's sound, watches the sun glint on the wings, observes it proceed, watches the jet trail, keeps watching the jet trail after the plane has disappeared. The airplane gets his undivided attention. When that same child is about three years old, he will look up, see the plane, say to himself, "Oh yeah, an airplane," and then look down and go about his business. By this time, he has learned to categorize the experience of watching and listening to the airplane so that he no longer *has* to watch and listen. Noticing an airplane and applying the category "airplane," he then withdraws his attention from his experience of the airplane and puts it somewhere else. The ability to do this enhances his efficiency. Almost all of us become more efficient in this way. Otherwise, we'd spend all our lives looking at airplanes.

The problem is that we begin to treat people, who are highly unpredictable phenomena, the same way that we treat the highly predictable phenomenon of an airplane flight. The result is that sometimes people we know do something new and unpredictable after we have stopped watching and are only manipulating a category they represent. We then end up missing a lot that is new in the world.

A child learning not to watch an airplane is an example of simple reductionism. Emotionally loaded reductionism, like little Stephen's conclusion in *The Downward Path to Wisdom* (the short story excerpted in Chapter 3), is the same kind of learning with feelings of hurt and anger mixed in. The emotionally-loaded reductionism of a child becomes the philosophy of life and world view of the adult.

Thus, category systems from the past eat us alive. They destroy our aliveness by capturing all of our attention so that we starve to death, without noticing our hunger for simple contact with people and everyday experience. After being sufficiently lost in the nest of categories, we never meet anyone new. We only meet representatives of people we used to know. *We learn to hate people for reminding us of stereotypes that existed in our own minds before we met them, and we never meet anyone new,* and we starve to death from loneliness.

Self-Image vs. Self

What are we talking about when we speak of our "selves"? What do the words mean with which we try to describe our so-called "selves"? My own self is indescribable. So is yours. My description of myself is not my self anymore than a description of a rose is a rose. As Tim Gallwey says in the *Inner Game of Golf:* "A self-image is only a picture of a real self. Just as a photograph is a two-dimensional representation of something three dimensional and cannot capture every detail or perspective of the object itself, our self-image can never encompass our true potential."[4]

Having an image of who we are and how we should behave is a great constraint on us. Escape from the mind happens in spite of, rather than because of, our self-image, whether it's a good one or a bad one. Anyone who thinks a good self-image is important is full of shit. If you have a psychotherapist who tells you that it is, go find another one.

The only way you can tell the truth when talking about your so-called "self" is to report it as an image you have. You are an imaginary person to yourself. You'd like for other people to imagine you the way you want them to. You spend a lot of time sculpting your image in the eyes and minds of others. It is an interesting game, but if it becomes the point of living it is a waste of life. It is in obedience to the rules of this game that people lose the playful freedom that had them start playing games in the first place. When you are talking *about* yourself, you can't be telling the truth about anything but an imagining you have.

Descriptive words evoke feelings that come and then go away. Thus, even when you speak honestly in any given moment, by describing what you are experiencing, it often becomes no longer true. This can be frustrating, but the truth of experience is naturally ephemeral. It's so fleeting, in fact, that language can't keep up with it. So, when you describe your experience, and the truth changes for you, you can be sure you have spoken the truth even though you also know that what you just said is no longer true.

A good example of this is people who "fall in love" but then have it go wrong for them. John loved Mary in 1986 more than his own life, and she loved him the same. In 1990 they got divorced. What happened in between? They were blissfully together for a three-day weekend in March, they made love seven times, they feasted on love and were happier than either could remember ever having been. They wanted to hold on to that remembered bliss. They wanted to do whatever they could to take care of each other and to express gratitude and work to keep that love alive. They didn't ever want that to change. Now and then they had some experiences together that didn't quite live up to that standard. Trying to make it all like it used to be eventually devolved into an obligation for which they began to resent each other. The wonderful beginning became a basis for comparison. John sits around in bars now listening to Hank Williams singing, "Why don't you love me like you used to do? Why do you treat me like a worn-out shoe?"

Tom Robbins said, in *Still Life with Woodpecker*, that the question of the age was "How do you make love stay?"[5] You don't. You let it come and go. Then there is a new opening for new love. Otherwise the space for love no longer exists, being occupied with ashes and bullshit.

When you speak descriptively about a present-tense experience, and it changes, you have spoken the truth. It's okay that it is no longer true. Don't worry about it. It is the way things are, and it is fine that they are that way. It's more fun and less boring than trying to keep track of everything. It's called freedom.

This experience of freedom is no big accomplishment at all to non-minded beings. Dogs run free. They don't have consciousness of freedom because they have nothing to measure it by, no unfreedom to compare it with, no ideals or images of perfect dogdom to hamper them unless they are particularly well-trained in obedience. Lucky for us, freedom stands out dramatically against the background of driving ourselves crazy with our minds, which, of course, we have to learn how to do in order to grow up. The possibility created by having been enslaved by a mind is that one can learn to appreciate freedom. When one has learned to appreciate freedom, the world becomes a place of creation, rather than a mind-smothered place. The mind becomes the enemy that has been defeated and made an ally. ⌐

THE SONG OF THE BLUE UNICORN
A Fairy Tale by Carol Mason*

ONCE UPON A TIME there was a Blue Unicorn. It had large blue eyes and a long blue tail and a fine blue horn. The Blue Unicorn had been alive for as long as it could remember, and for as long as it could remember it had never seen another creature such as itself.

The Blue Unicorn lived in the land which it came to know as the Land of Bright Meadows, where it pranced in the grass and frisked in the flowers and played with all the meadow creatures. Happy were the days of the Blue Unicorn and safe were its nights.

But there was a gap somehow, between the Blue Unicorn and the Land of Bright Meadows in which it lived. Something which the land had and the Blue Unicorn had not — a sound in the air of the Land of Bright Meadows that the Blue Unicorn half-heard, half-felt, but could never quite understand. A green and whispering sound — like the sound of a seed softly stirring its way from Winter to Spring.

*Copyright 1965 by Carol Mason.

"What is that sound?" asked the Blue Unicorn.

"It is the sound of our singing," replied the Land of Bright Meadows.

"Of what do you sing?" asked the Blue Unicorn.

"We live and grow towards the sun,
To wake is easy, to sleep is fun,
Life is good and life is long —
Because we live we sing our song."

"We sing the Song of Living," replied the Land of Bright Meadows.

The Blue Unicorn listened once more and then tried to sing the Song of Living. But the only sound that it could make was a crackling, papery sound — like the sound of a dry husk peeling from a bulb. And the Land of Bright Meadows murmured in sympathy and wonder.

"Teach me to sing," said the Blue Unicorn.

"Our song is ours, you must find your own," replied the Land of Bright Meadows. "We are we and you are alone."

"Somewhere, somewhere there must be another creature just like me who can teach me to sing," said the Blue Unicorn.

The Blue Unicorn left the Land of Bright Meadows and came to the Land of Deep Forest where forest creatures nestled and burrowed and the tall trees stretched dark above. The Blue Unicorn wandered in and out of the damp moss and dappled bracken towards the heart of the Land of Deep Forest, and as it did so, it heard again the sound it now knew to call 'singing' — a brown and velvet sound, like the sound of a root delving for water.

"Of what do you sing?" asked the Blue Unicorn.

"Toward the sun we live and grow,
Secrets of sap and seed we know.
We cannot share what we have learnt—
Knowledge won is knowledge earnt."

"We sing the Song of Wisdom," replied the Land of Deep Forest.

The Blue Unicorn listened once more and then tried to sing the Song of Wisdom. But the only sound that it could make was the sound of a sigh — like the sound a leaf makes as it flutters from Autumn to Winter. And the Land of Deep Forest rustled in sympathy and wonder.

"Teach me to sing," said the Blue Unicorn.

"Our song is ours, you must find your own," replied the Land of Deep Forest. "We are we and you are alone."

"Somewhere, somewhere there must be another creature just like me who will teach me to sing," said the Blue Unicorn.

And the Blue Unicorn left the Land of Deep Forest and came to the Land of Bare Mountains where vast and ancient chasms divided each lofty range, where no tree grew and no bird flew and no shelter was there from storm or night. Higher and higher climbed the Blue Unicorn, struggling to reach the highest peaks, and as it did so, it heard again the sound that it now knew to call 'singing' — a triumphant, ringing sound, like the sound a pinnacle makes as it pierces the wide sky.

"Of what do you sing?" asked the Blue Unicorn.

"We live and grow toward the sun,
Alone and proud, the weak we shun.
Fearing nothing, our hearts embrace
Both grief of time and joy of space."

"We sing the Song of Freedom."

The Blue Unicorn listened once more and then tried to sing the Song of Freedom. But the only sound that it could make was a painful, moaning sound — like the sound the wind makes as it searches bleak crags for somewhere to rest. And the Land of Bare Mountains echoed in sympathy and wonder.

"Teach me to sing," said the Blue Unicorn.

"Our song is ours, you must find your own," replied the Land of Bare Mountains. "We are we and you are alone."

"Somewhere, somewhere there must be another creature just like me who will teach me to sing," said the Blue Unicorn.

And the Blue Unicorn left the Land of Bare Mountains and came to the Land of White Sands where not rain nor wind nor cloud ruffled the glowing air. And the Blue Unicorn entered into the sound it now knew to call 'singing' — a sound as full and as rich as the best of the Blue Unicorn's blue heart — the sound of silence.

"Of what do you sing?" asked the Blue Unicorn.

And the Land of White Sands replied:

"Under the sun we rest and know
While we are still, all else can grow
Silence dwells behind each sound;
In that we trust, our song we've found."

"We sing the Song of Peace."

The Blue Unicorn listened once more and then tried to sing the Song of Peace, but the Land of White Sands shivered with sympathy and wonder to hear not singing — but the deep and awful sound of despair.

"Teach me to sing," said the Blue Unicorn.

"Our song is ours, you must find your own," replied the Land of White Sands. "We are we and you are alone."

The Blue Unicorn speckled the white sand with blue tears and said:

"Somewhere, somewhere there must be another creature just like me who will teach me to sing."

And the Blue Unicorn left the Land of White Sands and came to the Land of Clear Waters which stretched shimmering to the edge of the world. Weary was the Blue Unicorn, with a deep weariness that made the very marrow of its bones to ache. And the Blue Unicorn rested a while at the Land of Clear Waters, listening to the gentle, lapping sound it now knew to call 'singing.'

The Blue Unicorn lowered its head to drink, but as it did so, it quivered with sudden wonder and joy to see in the water below another creature — just like itself!

"O teach me to sing!" cried the Blue Unicorn. Then its heart stopped to hear that the creature below had cried even so. And the cry was followed by silence.

Then the Land softly sang:

> *"As the blue of our waters is the blue of the sky*
> *Your own self you see, to yourself you cry.*
> *And what you would learn you always knew*
> *For you are us and we are you.*
> *We are the Waters of Love*
> *Of us we bid you to drink.*
> *With us we bid you to sing."*

And the song of the Blue Unicorn was exactly the same and quite unlike every song that was ever sung. ⌒

13

FREEDOM

I'M IN LOVE with the independent being that's in the background, witnessing the mind's moralism and thoughts and principles and ideas and experiences. All human problems occur within the context of this witness being, who views the body's experiences, the ongoing panoply of life, and the mind itself. This being includes everything we ever thought, and everyone we used to think we were, but is not limited to those thoughts and images. When we adopt the perspective of that witness as our own, that is, when each of us considers ourselves to *be* that witness, we then have the freedom to use all of the "MEs" in our minds' "images" section to make happen whatever we want to make happen in our lives. And this new, wider sense of who we are leaves us being more creative and more willing to fly by the seat of our pants.

That witness sits quietly, being the context within which the mind struggles and oppresses itself. The mind's primary interest is control, while the witness is more interested in revelation than in control. The witness is always there, but often when people first come to see me in therapy, suffering from the oppression of their own minds, that witness is so surrounded by mind-stuff that both the being and the mind are dying.

This witness-creator-being, which includes within itself the unique case history personality, operates differently than your average Jo. For example, this being would only be in a marriage as a matter of choice and not as a matter of security. She wouldn't be engaged in a relationship based on a promise from the other person not to hurt her feelings. That expanded-to-the-width-of-the-witness being is capable of saying "I'm here on this planet for experiencing and I want to be a creator, not a victim. I'm willing to learn and keep learning. I am willing to experiment with life. I am more interested in discovery than carefulness. I can depend on my alertness more than my certainty that I'm right. I am more interested in learning than in protection."

At this level of consciousness, it doesn't matter a lot whether the social arrangements experimented with are monogamous, polygamous, communist, capitalist, or socialist. It doesn't matter whether the person in bed next to us is a stranger or is the person we've slept with for most of the past ten years. The encounter of two beings is what love is. At this level of being where love is, one-night stands are just as good as lifetime relationships. The place where energy is simply playing with our bodies, or where the beings that we are play with each other, is a nice place, and you can go there with anybody, any time.

My Friends

I stand as one among many. A whole bunch of us now know that it is more fun to be alive than to be right. We have lost our minds and come to our senses enough times to know what the goal is.

When we are at our best we are radicals — meaning we get at the root of things. We create. We tell the truth. We get off on destroying pretense. We have a technology of creation based on giving up lies and starting over again, over and over again. We can teach by example.

We are an antidote to the poison of conventional education we have all received. We wish to make us all more like animals. We are still angry, but we are less angry than the calm-looking phonies who have control of the bomb. We are less blinded by anger than your average pathetic rationalizing miserable bastard, engaged in the normal politics of experience. We are the new teachers. We are out to save the world. We are against politeness because politeness kills. Politeness and diplomacy are responsible for more suffering and death than all the crimes of passion in history. Fuck politeness. Fuck diplomacy. Tell the truth.

I have one of the best jobs in the world. The opportunity given me to contribute to other people by listening to their struggle between being and mind is a great gift, because it gives me the opportunity to practice my own ongoing liberation. When I'm operating out of that "thank you for letting me in on your life," I'm a great therapist. When I'm paying attention with honor and with interest, I never have to think of what to say. Whatever comes out of me doesn't seem to come from me. It comes from us. When speaking comes out of listening rather than the reverse, I am liberated from my mind just as much as they are from theirs.

Missionary Work: The Organizing Principle of the Newly Saved
It should come as no surprise that I recommend helping other people as a method of staying awake. Since memorizing the *idea* of liberation kills liberation, you have to do something other than memorize and remember to keep being liberated. What keeps you liberated is interaction with other people interested in staying in contact with their fundamental nature as beings, and being honored by the opportunity they provide you when they allow you to contribute to them in this way.

So the first thing you want to do to keep alive is find a "missionary group" that is going about the business of liberation from the mind. The future of your therapy and of therapy itself is in community. A community organized around people helping themselves and other people be liberated from their minds is your best bet. These groups provide a service not only to each other, but to people who could well use their services but don't know it yet. The kind of group I recommend is one in which the people don't seem to be in too big of a hurry.

Yuppie Salvation: Relief from the Anxiety of Too Many Choices
We are all very busy these days. Technology run amok creates new possibilities by the dozens every day. It's a lot of fun, but we wear ourselves out trying to experience *everything* when everything is too plentiful to be experienced.

You and I are always missing something and wishing we weren't, and always feeling that *real* life is where we're not. Whenever we are doing anything we are *missing* everything else. Commercials in our own minds constantly whisper to us of something else we should be doing: watching TV, playing the guitar, going out to eat, playing video games, sitting on the front deck, sitting on the back deck, eating food, drinking alcohol, smoking dope, having a meeting, playing golf, running, working, etc. This whisper goes on day and night: a background conscientiousness that bugs the shit out of us. It says, "While you are doing this, you are missing all the rest." How do you calm down enough to re-contact being in the midst of all this?

I constantly fret about books and movies I miss, or am missing, or might miss, or should not miss. How much more is there to know than I will ever learn? It boggles the mind. I am greedy — I am hysterically greedy — I am so impatient, I am hardly here at all. There is already *more to be learned than can be learned.*

The accumulation of other human beings' creative products now available to us has amounted to more than we can ever use. It's pointless for us to avail ourselves of all learning opportunities, or of all activities of interest. We freeze up from trying not to die in too many ways. We have to let go of possibilities for the future as well as memories from the past. *We burn out from holding on to possibilities for the future, in just the same way we deaden ourselves by trying to hold on to and live up to images and values from the past.* We work just as hysterically to keep the future alive as we do when we try to keep the past alive.

We are paralyzed at the point of choice: we cannot say "yes" for all the "no"s required in order to do so. We can't orient ourselves without dreams, and we choke the life out of ourselves when we are trapped in them.

We even have dreams about what never was but could be,

and then compare how we live to those ideal dreams. We need dreams to furnish ourselves with ideas for action, but remain paralyzed in inaction. On the one hand we get a little peace now and then, when we escape our mind's constant evaluation, and on the other we need that constant reassessment to get on in the world and to get the things we want. Then, when we do create something, it never lives up to the dream from which it came. Buddha was right, the suffering is built in. If we don't rescue ourselves from our intense attachment to too many expectations, we'll continue to be controlled by the anxiety of multiple choices — going crazy from too many options. Dreamjam. We'll go numb from possibilities. Every time you make up your mind to say yes to one thing you have to decide at the same time to say no to forty others. Saying no to forty possibilities just to say yes to one is a pain in the ass.

How did we get to dreamjam? Does it have anything to do with what is real? How did we get so far removed from necessity to become completely lost in the conversations of the mind? Resistance to limiting the future by commitment — to one project to the exclusion of others, or to one person to the exclusion of others — is the sickness of our time. The mind wants either the certainty of its own tradition, or it wants the hope of limitless accomplishment in the future. Thus the mind imposes limits and hates limitations. We are hoist on our own petards. We are damned if we do and damned if we don't, forever trapped by our attempts to revivify the past or *vivify* a new future that excludes other possibilities.

How do we rescue ourselves? We have to acknowledge the

built-in nature of our suffering — accept both the voice that tells us we're not doing enough *and* the fact that we will never be able to do all that we want to do — and act anyway. We must accept and affirm the sacrifice of alternatives and take the pain. There are no short cuts.

As I mentioned before, when we humans figured out the idea of hauling off our refuse it saved more lives than anything else in the history of medicine. We can do the same now with the garbage of the mind. Expectations, plans, and hopes for the future will still voice themselves, but instead of becoming overwhelmed, we can focus on choosing a few and discarding the rest, and then acting only on what we have chosen. The good news is that when we choose, act, and let ourselves be, the yammering voice of infinite choice fades. It may still be there, but its hold over us dies. We need to know how to let all the good and bad images go, whether they are from the past or from the future. And we need to let all the good and bad feelings associated with those images die. Let not only anger, hurt and bad feelings die, but let love die too. When either love *or* hate dies, love can be born again. That is particularly good news, and may be what Jesus was talking about. It's probably the meaning of the Resurrection: love dies to be reborn. When we let die our attachments to remembrances, expectations, moral imperatives, evaluations, comparisons, self-images, beliefs about how others should behave, ideals, and even romance, we make ourselves clearings for love's rebirth. Love is being wide open to the present, not blocked by nostalgia for some memory of the past or anticipation of some new love of the future. Love of another person happens only in a moment. Love is never having to say anything.

How do we die to all the emotional attachments of the mind? The job in staying alive is always to detach ourselves from our concepts; particularly our concepts of *how things are, who we are* and *how we should behave.*

How Things Are

None of us are ever really looking at how it is out there. I have my view of "how things are." You have your view of "how things are." We have to depend, in case of disagreement, on another nut like ourselves (a friend, therapist, or judge) with some other view of "how things are" to arbitrate for us. And it's no accident that "arbitrate" comes from the same root word as arbitrary. The truth is, none of us ever know what is going on. We just agree to have beliefs in common as a way of keeping things together. It's amazing how we copy each other's views so well that we can have such organized living. It's also pretty amazing how groups of us are willing to defend to the death our interpretations against other groups' interpretations, or punish "crooked" interpretations within our own groups. It's amazing because there is really no way to tell if "out there" is out there or not. But whatever it is, it's all created by individual beings, who then get together and agree what to call it. Assuming that seeing, hearing, smelling and so on are chemical reactions in organisms, then each individual organism, as I argued in Chapter One, is the creator of the world. We have to see if our creations agree with each other by doing a lot of cross-checking in the course of growing up. Even then, just at the perceptual level, it's hard to get agreement among people about what the world really is and what it is like. Science is a formal attempt to agree on the criteria we are willing to accept as a basis of agreement, in advance of any agreements. In that way the laws and agreed-upon assumptions of science are just like the laws and agreed-upon assumptions of the U.S. Constitution. We humans have spent a lot of time and energy for the past several thousand years trying to get clear on our agreements about perception and our agreements about value.

People kill each other by the minute over what it all means. The solution probably won't ever be just having everyone believe the same thing. Instead of working toward commonality of views, we need to work toward common acceptance of the principle of variety. We need a variety of ways to look at how things are, because ultimately we have a better chance of supporting each other with a lot of ways of viewing things. It may feel less secure than if everyone agrees on what is true, but the feeling of security is just that — a feeling, not the real thing. Less secure is often more reliable. If there is *not* enough variety preserved in the gardens of illusion about "how things are," then some version of *1984* totalitarianism will come true. This scenario is almost as shitty as the more tragic one of being blown away or dying of poison. I think communal acceptance of a variety of illusions, with less murderous defense of belief, is a better solution.

Beliefs about Who We Think We Are
In order to render ourselves fit for such a community of acceptance of multivariant weirdos, we need to destroy who we think we are. Who we generally think we are is our "reputations to

ourselves." We think we are our memory of our past actions, attitudes, and remembered records. That's not who we are, but it takes a lot of learning and energy to discover that, just as it took a lot of energy and learning to build that picture for ourselves in the first place. The energy required for being who we really are — full persons — comes from burning all the bullshit beliefs you built your mind out of. Fortunately, since one's mind is a constant bullshit generator, there is an unlimited supply of fuel.

When we are trying to protect and preserve our image of who we are, much of our time is spent in worrying. When we try to improve our image, much of our time is spent in fantasy. A lot of us get to the place where worry or fantasy are the only two choices we have. You go crazy when worry and fantasy are your only two options.

Death of a Salesman's Willie Loman, who commits suicide as a last-ditch effort to match his own self-image, is a good example of the despair of gradually falling into fantasy out of worry, and cutting loose from experience. In order to survive with enough sanity not to kill ourselves, we must learn to get lost in another place. That place is experience. We need to get lost in experience and entranced by just living and getting around and doing physical things in the world.

Activity in one dimension of the awareness continuum allows for rest in the others. The dimension of the awareness continuum in which worrying and fantasy reside is called the mind. The two other dimensions of awareness which I labeled earlier are, respectively, "what you notice *in* your body right now" and "what you notice *outside* your body right now." These two other aspects are categorizeable as "all present-tense experience." The good life is being able to play in all areas of the awareness continuum with full concentration and to alternate where you put your attention at will. Playing golf, for example, gives some worriers a chance to get lost in something else other than worry. It doesn't help if they start worrying about the golf game, but it helps a lot if they get lost in the game, rather than the worry.

A major focus of any worthwhile psychotherapy is an attempt to reawaken this ability to get lost in experience, by reawakening noticing. One of the first things to notice is that worry and fantasy, which are twins, have captured all of your attention. The second thing to notice is that when you aren't worrying or fantasizing there is still something left.

Along with worry comes "feeling bad." Some people become gifted in getting conscious of feeling bad. Feeling bad on purpose, hamming up feeling bad and deepening the gloom to notice more about how one does it can lead to learning how to love the blues. Allowing yourself to feel bad gets you over it, particularly if at the same time you unload a bunch of secrets. If you are worried your mother-in-law will find out you smoke pot, tell her. You won't have that worry anymore, you'll feel better, you'll get some new problems, and you may find out that more is permissible that you've ever imagined.

Sometimes a kind of deep brooding becomes enjoyable, like hearing a deep bass note. When you really get into the blues you start feeling good. When you stop resisting worrying, worry becomes less worrisome, and willingness to let it happen ultimately ruins the blues. They run their course. Being able to come back from the blues and act in the world again happens naturally.

Getting depressed is fine and expectable and probably helpful. Before there were too many social workers and psychotherapists, everyone expected to get the blues now and then. They also expected to get over them, to get creative and renewed now and then, and to get lost in their work in the world. Regularly alternating what captures our concentration is good for our health. The ability to get absorbed, in gloom, in fantasy, *or* in being in the world so much that we lose track of who we are is a great power.

Who is it that gets lost at these times when we seem so absorbed we forget everything else? Actually, it's not really a who, it's a what. What gets lost is the voiceover we are used to calling ourselves. We "lose ourselves" in some mental activity or task in the world and in so doing create the possibility of discovering the self that's left when that false self is gone. We find out who we *really* are when we lose "ourselves" through concentration.

I'm saying two things about this: first, it is of vital importance that you learn to be lost both in experience and in your mind, but not permanently, so that you get the avenue of escape each offers from the other. Secondly, when you get lost in what you're concentrating on, the "you" that gets lost track of is not who you are. Who you are is the "I lost track of myself" being, before you noticed you had lost track of yourself. Who you are is the concentration. *Who we are* is the being without any identity, within whom the mind and the perceiver and the reactor to experience reside. *Who we are* is a space within which two kinds of playing occur: experience and fantasy about experience. We are not our experience, and we are not our fantasies about our experience, past, present, or future. We are the theatre in which those things occur.

Who we actually are is about the same kind of being everyone else is: a fantastic electrical biochemical machine constantly creating reality out of being alive.

In order to be fully alive, we have to constantly shed attachment to ideas *from* the past and *about* the future. The biggest, fattest idea to ditch first, in order to be creative, is the idea of who we are.

One way we shed attachment to who we think we are is to face death. Michael Zimmermann, a modern existentialist philosopher writing about Heidegger, explains that what allows us to rescue ourselves from our own egos is that we can see we are going to die:

> Revelation of my finitude severs constricting bonds to the past and frees me for the future. If I accept that death is always possible, the complacency of egoism disappears. Since I am here only for a brief time, there is no better moment than the present for choosing my own limited possibilities. Too often, I assume that my 'moment of truth' lies in the future and excuses the slackness of my existence.[1]

Psychotherapy works like a death announcement: like a doctor telling you that you have only six months to live. The message is "You're not going to live forever and you won't be able to do most of the things you want to do before you die and there is very damn little you're in charge of anyway." If the client gets that message, it can considerably shorten the length of time it takes to conduct psychotherapy.

The "giving up" that comes with the acceptance of one's own death and the futility of proving one's worth allows for freedom. Psychotherapy is for becoming free and creative. A freely functioning, creative being is one who has "severed constricting bonds to the past." When the mind discovers that the past is dead, and furthermore, that all is dying, energy is eventually freed up for some project toward the future. But this freed-up energy lacks the previous drivenness and desperation of the ego trying to survive.

Beliefs about How We Should Behave

Beliefs about how we should behave are all bullshit. There is no way for us to do the right thing. Thinking we are doing the right thing is a part of the illusion of being in control. When you place your faith in your own judgment, you place your faith in your judge. You get to believing that your judge is who you are. Catholic parochial education is a perfect model for teaching children that their superegos are who they are. Investment in that belief is the antithesis of healthy aliveness. As a psychotherapist, curing Catholicism is one of the biggest challenges I have. If I put that on an insurance form as a diagnosis, the insurance company won't pay for my services, so I use terminology from another model: "anxiety neurosis." One of the worst and most resistant strains of anxiety neurosis is implanted by the Catholic Church because they teach young children that the most important thing in life is being right. Almost all of South America is an exemplary backwater of Catholicism. The Catholic Church is by no means the only source of this teaching, it's just that they are particularly good at it. But we all suffer from varying degrees of this "catholic" disease.

It is a milestone in growing up to get this: there is no way to be right. There is no right way to behave. There is no way to know you have done the right thing. There is no way to know if what you are planning to do is right. If you got the abortion, was it the right thing? If you had the baby, was it right? You do what you do. You did what you did. The right and the wrong of it are not worth spending a lot of time on.

Where to Look for People Who Are Interested in the Truth
When we commit ourselves to something beyond the campaign for righteousness, we are missionaries for liberation. To return to my original point, we then need to find a missionary group of people who are working to save people from their beliefs. In joining such a group to help save others from their minds we may get saved occasionally from our own.

One of the benefits of having a mind is that this phenomenon occurs: once you know what you are looking for, it starts to show up. These people are all over the place and the ones you find will probably be other than the ones I mention but I will mention a few anyway.

Landmark Educational Foundation
Trainings that for a long time were being led by Werner Erhard and Associates are still being led by the associates. These trainings

involve conversations and life designs which get into the details of the technology of creation. These people are working on the integration of Eastern and Western ways of being human, operating from the stand that human beings can learn to be fascinated by playing with their lives, rather than trying to be good children and gain favor and get someone to take care of them in exchange for being good. Some of the "followers" of this group are "true believers" and therefore full of shit, but you are not going to find a perfect group. We are all still working on something we don't know everything about.

Transcendental Meditation
People at the TM organization teach a great system for settling down deeply so that noticing gets born again. Many of them are a little too holy and pure and they don't know shit about how to handle anger as expression, but TM is a great practice to learn, and the people are on a mission to help everyone re-contact the nourishment of being.

Telling the Truth Workshops
My friends and colleagues and I run a nine-day workshop called Telling the Truth. Here you can find support in telling the truth. The whole workshop involves nine days of residential work and six months of once-a-week follow-up group meetings. If you want to know more details, call or write.

Supporting the Support You Already Have
Give this book to your therapist. Give this book to your spouse.

Give this book to your friends. Give this book to members of any current group you are in. Start your own telling the truth group. Once you get started, write us, and we will see what we can do to help. Your real support is wherever the truth is being told. ~

THE FINAL LOWDOWN

THE FULL PATH OF GROWTH from birth to maturity consists of: *1.* the birth of being, *2.* the growth of the mind, *3.* a period of domination of the being by the mind, *4.* liberation of the being from the mind, and finally *5.* a mind used by the being. Having told the truth enough, the being becomes liberated from its own mind. Having told the truth enough, the being takes charge of its mind, rather than remaining suppressed by its mind. The period of liberation of the being from domination by its mind involves many experiences of disorientation and then reorientation. Reorientation of the being to sources other than the mind is based on being in touch with one's own body and noticing things in the world. During these times the opportunity for freedom occurs — freedom from the previously developed network of thought. *Thinking* becomes merely something else to *notice and use* when one has become reoriented to experience. Thinking loses its prior status as a the primary ruler and jailkeeper of being and becomes more like the chauffeur.

Being trapped in the jail of the mind is a disease called moralism. All relief from moralism is temporary because there is no permanent cure. The use of drugs like alcohol can provide short-term, temporary relief, like using Alka Seltzer for an upset stomach. Telling the truth is more like a time-release capsule that lasts for days or weeks, or like an exercise and diet program that works to improve your strength and resistance over a period of time.

We are all moralists. The more moralistic we are, the more hysterical we are. The more hysterical we are, the further away from experience we wish to be. So we go as far away from nasty old disorganized experience as we can get, which means as far toward an abstract, external point of reference as we can.

We have been systematically taught hysteria in the form of moralism. Many teachers think the point of education is to learn rules and learn to value them highly. Well-known moral hysterics like Jerry Falwell have generated agreement among thousands of people who are comforted by his ability to forcefully recreate this preference for principles over aliveness. The moral hysteria of Geraldine Ferraro or Walter Mondale or Michael Dukakis or Jesse Jackson is not an alternative, but another form of the same thing. Liberal hysterics are not different from reactionary hysterics.

The character structure of one's personality — that is, the stability and configuration and intensity of one's value system — is actually independent of the values held. "Shouldists" are like sadists, and they live amongst all belief systems. Shoulding on yourself and others is like shitting on yourself and others.

Integrity, wholeness, at-one-ness, is the opposite of moralism. Having integrity is the opposite of being moral. If one has integrity, one doesn't need morals. People with integrity operate with rules of thumb, not morals. Integrity both results from and is a manifestation of telling the truth. Integrity is not a total cure for the disease of moralism, but significantly reduces its negative effects.

Willingness

Being willing is more important than being right. Paul Tillich called this willingness "the courage to be,"[1] and was careful to differentiate it from bravery due to a strong will. We do not need "will power," we need willingness. Will power is at the heart of the life-poisoning systems we are sick of and sick from. Awareness of that being that exists underneath and prior to the rules of order, and identification with that being, is the way out of the trap. That being is always willing. The self-pushing and self-condemnation that comes out of "letting your conscience be your guide" is a vicious circle. *Don't* let your conscience be your guide. Follow any goddamned thing else but your conscience.

Albert Camus said that the question of the age is whether or not to commit suicide: that is, is life worth the effort? Are you willing to live or do you judge that it's not worth the effort? I say the important question is "Who's asking? Who asked you? Where is the question coming from?" The judge who has poisoned experience, through the alienation which judgment itself represents, wishes now to make a judgment of whether life is worth the price, since, in his judgment, life never lives up to its billing. Such an arrogant question: "Is life worth the trouble?" When it is answered in the negative and a person commits suicide, the judge who made the decision is preserved at the expense of the being who grew him.

Being right is not the most important thing in life. If it was, you might as well kill yourself. Being willing is what counts. If we are willing, we are fools, as any good mind will tell you. Exactly. Fools rush in and learn all kinds of things angels will never know.

Grace

The experience of having one's vicious circle of judgment broken in upon is called "grace" in Christian theology. The event that brings about the break is called a Christ event. The historical Christ broke in on history in the same way in which an individual mind gets broken in on. A Christ event is any event that shakes you out of your conceptual do-loop and hands you back your awareness. God is the sense of willingness. God is the involuntary nervous system in your body that keeps everything running regardless of what you think. You relate to God by being aware. You relate to God by becoming who you are, which is an awareness. You relate to God by becoming God. When you are most aware of relating to another being you are most in touch with God. God is the collective involuntary nervous systems of people. God is the ineffable experience of awareness of being related to another. God is receiving yourself and another person in being, as you are, in any moment. God is the eternal split-second sound-light being. God is when what is so, objectively, is subjectively experienced. Awareness is the key practice for the experience of Godness. What I think Kierkegaard meant, when he said "a person who relates to another person and relates also to that relationship relates thereby to God,"[2] is that a consciousness relating consciously to another consciousness relates to consciousness

its own self. We all (Buddhists, Christians, Hindus, psychotherapists, lovers) agree on this. Catholics, of course, with the exception
of Thomas Merton, are not Christians. Moslems are generally a
bunch of moralistic assholes who might as well be Catholic.

Being willing does not mean you never play the game of
judgment. Being aware does not mean you have no conscience.
The difference is in flex. As you may have noticed, I particularly
love playing the game of judgment and condemnation of the
Catholic church. I love my experience of rightness and righteous
indignation about those poor assholes. I like the experience just
like any other righteous prick, Catholics included. The difference is I have more to sustain me than my beliefs, mostly from
luck rather than virtue on my part. I have been lucky. These poor
suffering bastards who never grew out of pre-adolescent moralism, that make up the iron-fisted keepers of the rules the world
over, believe in their beliefs and will kill rather than face dying to
their beliefs. Priests and generals and rigid revolutionaries are in
need of Christ events for delivery from the deadly seriousness of
their games.

The dirty little secret is out of the bag now. Your conscience *is*
the devil. The revolution of our times is the revolution of consciousness. The government to be overthrown is the government
of conscience, with its bureaucracy of moralism. Conscience in-
hibits being. We are developing our awareness to beat the devil.

Everyone knows intuitively that the bullshit moralism and
rules of good behavior of official religions have nothing whatsoever to do with the spiritual experience the religion is based upon.
How we should behave is really an unanswerable question. The

closest thing to an answer is be willing, and see what happens. Most of us might be willing to try that if we could be sure everyone else wasn't. We make up rules and sell them to other people and their children to protect our own asses.

The truth is this: We grow up. We grow old. We die. We all do that, and how we do it doesn't matter much. We all have to do about the same thing anyway. Believing we are doing the right thing is the centerpiece of our illusion of control of this process where we, in fact, have no real control. Beliefs are only useful as toys. Loving a belief is like loving a teddy bear. Defending beliefs as though they were sacred only demonstrates your stupidity.

Dylan Thomas' poem *Lament* is about growing up, growing old, and dying.[3] The manner of death, in the end, is death by virtue. Being killed by virtue is by far the commonest cause of death. Death is nature's way of telling you you ought to let up on yourself. By the time you get the message, of course, it's too late. This poem is about an old man looking back on his life. Dylan Thomas wrote it for his father when his father was dying.

Lament

When I was a windy boy and a bit
And the black spit of the chapel fold,
(Sighed the old ram rod, dying of women),
I tiptoed shy in the gooseberry wood,
The rude owl cried like a telltale tit,
I skipped in a blush as the big girls rolled
Ninepin down on the donkeys' common,
And on seesaw sunday nights I wooed

Whoever I would with my wicked eyes,
The whole of the moon I could love and leave
All the green leaved little weddings' wives
In the coal black bush and let them grieve.

When I was a gusty man and a half
And the black beast of the beetles' pews,
(Sighed the old ram rod, dying of bitches),
Not a boy and a bit in the wick-
Dipping moon and drunk as a new dropped calf,
I whistled all night in the twisted flues,
Midwives grew in the midnight ditches,
And the sizzling beds of the town cried, Quick! —
Whenever I dove in a breast high shoal,
Wherever I ramped in the clover quilts,
Whatsoever I did in the coal-
Black night, I left my quivering prints.

When I was a man you could call a man
And the black cross of the holy house,
(Sighed the old ram rod, dying of welcome),
Brandy and ripe in my bright, bass prime,
No springtailed tom in the red hot town
With every simmering woman his mouse
But a hillocky bull in the swelter
Of summer come in his great good time
To the sultry, biding herds, I said,
Oh, time enough when the blood creeps cold,

And I lie down but to sleep in bed,
For my sulking, skulking, coal black soul!

When I was a half of the man I was
and serve me right as the preachers warn,
(Sighed the old ram rod, dying of downfall),
No flailing calf or cat in a flame
Or hickory bull in milky grass
But a black sheep with a crumpled horn,
At last the soul from its foul mousehole
Slung pouting out when the limp time came;
And I gave my soul a blind, slashed eye,
Gristle and rind, and a roarers' life,
And I shoved it into the coal black sky
To find a woman's soul for a wife.

Now I am a man no more no more
And a black reward for a roaring life,
(Sighed the old ram rod, dying of strangers),
Tidy and cursed in my dove cooed room
I lie down thin and hear the good bells jaw —
For, oh, my soul found a sunday wife
In the coal black sky and she bore angels!
Harpies around me out of her womb!
Chastity prays for me, piety sings,
Innocence sweetens my last black breath,
Modesty hides my thighs in her wings,
And all the deadly virtues plague my death!

Aliveness declines to virtue, which leads to death. For some, that death is the kind that comes when you start a worm farm. For others, that death is an ego death, and it makes room for the rebirth of aliveness. The dying that brings rebirth comes about as a result of learning how to tell the truth.

Marilyn Ferguson speaks of how we keep trying to use our poor little left brain faculty to keep up with what's going on and what comical pathetic creatures we are in the attempt. "Change and complexity always outrun our powers of description.... When the left brain confronts the nonlinear dimension, it keeps circling around, breaking wholes into parts, retracing its data, and asking inappropriate questions, like a reporter at a funeral. Where, when, how, why? We have to inhibit its questions for the moment, suspend its judgment, or we cannot 'see' the other dimension, any more than we can see both perspectives of an optical illusion staircase at the same time — or be swept away by a symphony while analyzing the composition."[4] We are all that kind of left-brain-minded fools. We are all jerks, running on unfinished, old-timey, remembered experience, and at the direction of out-moded models of the mind. It's how we operate. It's our nature. It's how we all are. Denying that makes you a spastic. Affirming that makes you just a regular jerk. This is the era of the takeover of the world by spastics anonymous.

Members of spastics anonymous have given up wasting time trying to prove they're not jerks. Anyone stupid enough to have faith in his or her own judgment is a spastic, and the biggest damned fool of all.

We evoke feelings from the past by either remembering or

wishing. Wishing and remembering are attempts to stay alive, enlivened with feelings we choose to re-experience. Wishing and remembering are great fun. When we are remembering, for a while, we can re-evoke feeling. We get a chance to experience over again some pleasant experience we once had, and we have some sense of control over, and distance from, what we are remembering. But these re-experienced experiences peter out. They wear out partly because a long stay in heaven becomes hell. There is nothing to do in heaven. Everything is fixed. Nothing is broken. Everything is perfect. Heaven wears out. Nostalgia ain't what it used to be. So we turn our attention to the future to enact new fantasies based on pleasant experiences from the past. These fantasies about the future, based on the past, are the hope and hype we con ourselves with. Even if we get what we always wanted it never looks like we thought it would when it arrives. Success, therefore, leads to disillusionment. As Ecclesiastes says, "All is vanity and a striving after the wind." We end up in hell again. Our memories of heaven are what make hell possible. Only after years at this can we begin to give up faith in our own fantasies.

Then we discover the good news that hell makes heaven possible. "Abandon all hope, ye who enter here" was the sign marking Dante's entrance to Hell. But his trip into Hell was the beginning of the path to Heaven. "Abandon all hope, ye who enter here" is, in fact, the sign over the gateway to heaven. Each individual who matures to adulthood has to go through a late-adolescent hell and beyond. We have to learn to live lies. We need to be lost in a life of lying before the possibility of deliverance from hell presents itself. We have to learn how to avoid the moment and control our experience of the world through wishing, hoping, being lost in memory, lying and being lost in our minds. We have to be successful at this and despair of it and then escape from it without losing its advantages. All of that learning, all of that schooling in evaluation, was just a trick. After it has totally lost its value, it becomes of some use. We can dream as a game, fashion roles as a game, intellectualize as a game, and, most importantly, switch games when we want. Reality is neither heaven nor hell, it's a playground where you may get hurt at times. Spastics love soap operas because soap operas allow them to dream of not being such jerks. The jerks on soap operas are some people's idea of how to live the good life. Soap operas can't exist without lying, and vice versa. Spastics, in denying they are jerks, idealize jerkdom. What you get in place of aliveness is your average soap opera.

Lying

When you are lying, when you are keeping a secret, when you are withholding information *or* feelings in any moment, you are always doing that to protect something meaningless. You are usually protecting a memory to preserve a constant state of being. You can't see that what you are protecting is meaningless because the illusion of the self you are protecting blocks your view. When, through telling the truth, you destroy that illusion, you can then see that it was meaningless. Meaninglessness is of great value. When you finally get that who you *actually* are is empty and meaningless, it doesn't matter to you whether you are a jerk or not. There is where your power lives.

You may have an image of yourself as a "good" person. You may lie to keep from "hurting someone else's feelings." The someone else you are thinking of is even more ephemeral than the self-image you are protecting. The people you protect by lying are just as imaginary as the self-image you maintain when you lie to protect your self. This is the imaginary world of adolescence.

The odds are against growing beyond adolescence in our adolescent society. The odds favor most of us, most of the time, remaining polite impotent assholes who think we are special, but somehow don't get what we deserve. Most people feel like life hasn't lived up to its billing, hasn't turned out right, hasn't rewarded us appropriately. After a while, we give up thinking we are so hot and start dreaming about what could have been. This is the way life usually goes for most of us. We have all been waiting for a long time to grow beyond both these positive and negative self-images, and afraid to do so. Most of us never make it beyond adolescent hope and hype and disappointment. Wishing is a way to remove oneself from what is going on now. Hope springs eternal. Fuck hope. Hope is how most of us avoid growing up.

The power of positive thinking is the biggest load of bullshit of our day. Positive thinking is for negative people. With positive thinking and affirmations, we start from an image of ourselves as flawed, and try to use thinking as a strategy to make ourselves whole. Thinking is not the source of power. Being is the source of power. And in being, we are already whole.

The mind's work of survival becomes vanity when it goes

beyond helping *us* to survive, and becomes attached to the survival of our self-image. Besides that, we don't survive, either image or being, in the end, because we all die. Only our willingness to live at risk, and in the knowledge of death, can keep the mind from squeezing the life out of us before we die. The being within which the mind resides is willing to live and willing to die. The mind considers life and death to be important. The being considers life and death to be life and death. Surviving one's own mind is done by identifying oneself as the being one is and living out of that *being* rather than living out of the *image* of how we are or should be.

The mind grows out of being. What a great thing a mind is! When the mind is not imprisoning being, it's a marvelous thing. Its activities are fun. Fantasies are fun, predicting and controlling are fun, getting praise is fun, getting food is fun, organizing to produce results is fun, creating is fun. What justifies all of that work it took to develop a mind is that it turns out to be a great toy. I recommend having fun — although I don't recommend making another set of morals out of the philosophy of fun. It is okay *not* to get the most out of life. It is fine to let life happen and not get all the cookies. Getting the most out of life is too much work anyway. Anything worth doing is worth doing poorly. Let up on everything, including this.

So the big picture is this. The little teeny fire of life starts in a human being at conception and keeps burning until the end of life. The little fire of enlightenment follows about four or five or six months later, in the womb, and it also keeps on until the end. The slightly larger fire of learning starts shortly after the neonate gets outside, and burns regularly until almost the end. The little fire of abstract cognitive ability starts at about ten or eleven years of age and burns on until the end. The energy from all these fires, which are really one fire that has grown and spread, must be applied to something bigger than that one fire itself, or else the fire consumes itself; burns out.

Creating Bigger Problems for Fun

When we create some vision of the future to fill the gap left by "giving up," we create a new problem. When we say "yes" to some opportunity or project or activity, the choice requires dying to other options. You can only work on so many fantasies at once. Any inability to die to these other options cripples our aliveness to what we have chosen.

This book is for people who have suffered a few dis-illusionments already in their lives. That is, it's for everyone. The work it recommends, that of grouping together for liberation, is for people who have been saved and sold out again several times. Groups worth belonging to are people who support each other in staying in that area of insecurity and heightened experience and aliveness that threatens to kill your mind-made identity every day.

We know at least two things by the time we've been tempered by despair and become road-worthy facers of disillusionment:

1. There are no dependable truths. There are more or less dependable truths, and they change now and then.

2. There is one dependable source for common agreement. It is sensory data. We can and must assume that a direct report of sensory data is the closest we can get to shared common experience.

A simple language grows out of sensory experience. If we can speak to each other with Lone-Ranger-and-Tonto-like sensory language we can stay close to home-town reality. We can always return to that starting place when we get lost.

A mind is a web of abstractions, and once a mind has been grown and nurtured, the job becomes getting extricated from the web of abstraction and returning to home-town reality. It's not really reality, I know, but it is the best close-to-hand, agreed upon basis of interpretation we have. It is the only "reality" we've got. It's a hell of an assumption that your pain and my pain are the same, that your pleasure and my pleasure are alike, and that your perceptions match my perceptions, but this is the necessary basic level at which to begin. As a rule of thumb, if it's a choice between being lost in the stratosphere of thought or being dumb in down-home sensory reality, go home to sensate experience. Strange and mostly wonderful things happen to people when they are able to talk at the level of down-home reality.

People lost in the stratosphere of interpretations are lawyers and most people. People grounded in experience include some hillbillies, some golf pros, some other professional athletes, some Zen masters, some Gestalt therapists, most comedians, and some other people.

The doorway to becoming grounded in experience is called despair. Despair comes from the Latin root words *de* and *sperare* meaning "down from" and "hope." "Down from hope." The only hope is to give up hope. The only hope is a kind of hope through despair. Abandon all hope, give up romance, and learn the earth language. The truth is not some story about something that happened to you in the past. Telling stories about your memory of what happened may be entertaining for a while, but if that is all you can do it gets boring pretty fast. Truth can only be told if you are present in the telling and present to the person to whom you are talking. When I am describing to another person how things are, I am always describing how things are for me at the moment, or I am not telling the truth.

I can only tell the truth that is my truth at the moment. We don't have to agree with each other about how things are. We just have to listen to each other and get how things are for each other, now.

Last Words

Dean Rusk never beat his wife. He was a decent man. He was a liberal. He was head of the Ford Foundation. And as Secretary of State during the Vietnam war, he killed over a hundred thousand people in a useless, wasteful, unnecessary, stupid war. We would all be better off if he had beaten his wife. His time is passing with the turn of the century.

After a long period of romantic idealism, humanity is evolving a new way to live. Many are following the lead of great thinkers from previous centuries who knew, without using the term neurosis, that neurosis was a preoccupation with things of the mind, and that creation was the cure for it. For many centuries, certain poets, philosophers, and scientists have recognized another whole realm of being, which is living with just what's so, from the perspective of having nothing to lose and nothing to gain. We need not approach the world from preoccupation with thoughts and feelings about being good or bad, judging whether the world is good or bad enough for us. We can just as easily live out of being fascinated with the game of creation.

I believe that fascination with the game of creation is sufficient: that, in fact, it's the only game in town. And this wonderful game, once reserved for a few inspired perceivers, is now available to larger and larger numbers of people, because our culture itself is growing up. Our culture is growing to a place of young adulthood, growing beyond adolescence, for the first time in its history.

Personal Declarations of Independence are popping up like crazy. Honest people recognize and salute each other. These excerpts from Erica Jong's salute to Walt Whitman[5] articulate the possibility for all of us, finally, to grow up.

I love Erica Jong for the same reasons she loves Walt Whitman. These lines from her poem speak for all of us to each other.

Testament (Or, Ode to Walt Whitman)

loveroot, silkthread, crotch and vine...
　　　　　—Walt Whitman
I trust all joy.
　　　—Theodore Roethke

I, Erica Jong, in the midst of my life,
having had two parents, two sisters,
two husbands, two books of poems

& three decades of pain,

having cried for those who did not love me
& those who loved me — but not enough
& those whom I did not love —
declare myself now for joy.
There is pain enough to nourish us everywhere;
it is joy that is scarce.
There are corpses piled up to the mountains,
*   & tears to drown in*
*   & bile enough to swallow all day long.*

Rage is a common weed.

Anger is cheap.

Righteous indignation
*   is the religion of the dead*
*   in the house of the dead*
*   where the dead speak to each other*
*   in creaking voices,*
*   each arguing a more unhappy childhood*
*   than the other.*

Unhappiness is cheap.
*   Childhood is a universal affliction.*
*   I say to hell with the analysts of minus & plus,*
*   the life shrinkers, the diminishers of joy.*

I say to hell with anyone
*   who would suck on misery*

like a pacifier
in a toothless mouth
I say to hell with gloom

. . .

Gloom is cheap.
Every night the demon lovers
come with their black penises like tongues,
with their double faces,
& their cheating mouths
& their glum religions of doom.

Doom is cheap.
If the apocalypse is coming
let us wait for it in joy.

I resolve now for joy.

If that resolve means I must live alone,
I accept aloneness.

If the joy house I inhabit must be
a house of my own making,
I accept that making.

. . .

Dear Walt Whitman,
horny old nurse to pain
speaker of "passwords primeval,"
merit-refuser, poet of body & soul —

[285]

I scorned you at twenty
but turn to you now
in the fourth decade of my life,
having grown straight enough
to praise your straightness,
    & plain enough
    to speak to you plain
    & simple enough
    to praise your simplicity.

.   .   .

You were "hankering, gross, mystical, nude."
You astonish with the odor of your armpits.
Your cocked your hat as you chose:
    you cocked your cock —
    but you knew "the Me myself."

You believed in your soul
    & believing, you made others
    believe in theirs.

The soul is contagious.
    One man catches another's
    like the plague;
    & we are all patient spiders
    to each other.

If we can spin the joythread
    & also catch it —

if we can be sufficient to ourselves,
we need fear no entangling webs.

The loveroot will germinate.
The crotch will be a trellis to the vine,
& our threads will all be intermingled silk.

How to spin joy out of an empty heart?
The joy egg germinates even in despair.
Orgasms of gloom convulse the world;
& the joy seekers huddle together.

We meet on the pages of books & by beechwood fires.
We meet scrawled blackly in many-folded letters.
We know each other by free and generous hands.
We swing like spiders on each other's souls.

I, Brad Blanton, in the midst of my life,
having had three parents, three siblings,
four wives, four causes, four children,
& four decades of pain.
Having raged for those who did not love me
& those who loved me — but not enough
& those whom I did not love —
declare myself now for joy.

Help yourself. It's free. Pass it on. ⤝

FOR ADDITIONAL COPIES OF *Telling the Truth,* or information about the *Telling the Truth Workshop,* or to subscribe to the *Telling the Truth Community Newsletter,* please call:

1-800-EL TRUTH

Footnotes &
Quotation Credits

INTRODUCTION

1   Centers for Disease Control. Atlanta, GA: Department of Health, Education and Welfare, Public Health Services.

2   Nietzsche, Friedrich (1968). *Basic Writings of Nietzsche*. New York: The Modern Library.

3   Thomas, Hugh (1979). *A History of the World*. New York: Harper and Row.

4   Erikson, Erik (1963). *Childhood and Society*. New York: W.W. Norton & Company, Inc.

CHAPTER ONE

1   Bateson, Gregory (1979). *Mind and Nature*. New York: E.P. Dutton.

2   Asch, Soloman, *et al.* (1965). Journal of Abnormal and Social Psychology.

3   Perls, Frederick S. (1969). *Ego, Hunger, and Aggression*. New York: Random House.

4   Erikson, Erik (1962). *Young Man Luther*. New York: W.W. Norton & Company, Inc.

5   Ibid.

CHAPTER TWO

Quotation: Laing, R.D. (1976). *The Facts of Life*. New York: Pantheon Books.

1   Krishnamurti. *You Are the World*. New York: Harper and Row.

2   Ferguson, Marilyn (1981). *The Aquarian Conspiracy*. Los Angeles: Tarcher.

CHAPTER THREE

Quotation: cummings, e.e. (1972). *Complete Poems*. "anyone lived in a pretty how town" New York: Harcourt, Bruce, Jovanovich.

1   Yeats, William, B. (1940). *The Variorum Edition of Poems of W.B. Yeats*. New York: Macmilliam Company.

2   Porter, Katherine Anne (1969). "The Downward Path to Wisdom." *The Leaning Tower and Other Stories.* New York: Harcourt Brace Jovanovich.

CHAPTER FOUR

Quotation: Dylan, Bob. *My Back Pages.* New York: Alfred A. Knopf.

1   Stevens, John O. (1971). *Awareness: Exploring, Experimenting, Experiencing.* Real People Press.

2   Lawrence, D.H. (1964). *Complete Poems of D.H. Lawrence.* New York: Viking Press, Inc.

CHAPTER FIVE

Quotation: Emerson, Ralph Waldo (1951). *Self Reliance.* New York: Thomas Y. Crowell Company.

1   cummings, e.e. (1972). *Complete Poems.* New York: Harcourt, Bruce, Jovanovich.

2   Ibid.

3   Ibid.

CHAPTER SEVEN

Quotation: Keen, Sam (1986). *Faces of the Enemy: Reflections of the Hostile Imagination.* San Francisco: Harper & Row, Inc.

1   Brown, Norman O. (1971). *Life Against Death: The Psychoanalytical Meaning of History.* Middletown, CT: Wesleyan University Press.

2   Stevens, John O. (1971). *Awareness: Exploring, Experimenting, Experiencing.* Real People Press.

CHAPTER EIGHT

Quotation: Jans, Tom (1972). "Loving Arms." Almo Music Corp. (ASCAP).

1   Patterson, James and Kim, Peter. (1991) *The Day America Told the Truth.* New York: Prentice Hall.

2   Buber, Martin (1958). *I and Thou.* New York: Charles Scribner.

3   Kristofferson, Kris (1968). "When I Loved Her." Nashville, TN: BMG Music Publishing.

CHAPTER NINE

1   Nietzsche, Friedrich (1968). *Basic Writings of Nietzsche.* New York: The Modern Library.

CHAPTER TEN

Quotation: Heinlein, Robert A. (1963). *Stranger in a Strange Land.* New York: Putnam.

1 Steinbeck, John (1939). *The Grapes of Wrath.* New York: Viking Press.

CHAPTER ELEVEN

Quotation: Watts, Alan (1951). *The Wisdom of Insecurity.* New York: Pantheon Books.

1 Flournoy, Don (Ed.) (1970). *The New Teachers.* Chapter by William Coles. Jossey-Bass.

2 cummings, e.e. (1972). *Complete Poems.* New York: Harcourt, Bruce, Jovanovich.

3 Pantanjali, (J.H. Woods, Trans.) *Yoga Sutras.* Delhi: Motilal Banarsidass.

4 Gallwey, W. Timothy (1981). *The Inner Game of Golf.* New York: Random House, Inc.

5 Robbins, Tom (1980). *Still Life with Woodpecker.* New York: Bantam Books.

CHAPTER TWELVE

1 Mason, Carol (1965). *Song of the Blue Unicorn.*

CHAPTER THIRTEEN

1 Zimmermann, Michael E. (1981). *Eclipse of the Self.* Athens, London: Ohio University Press.

CHAPTER FOURTEEN

1 Tillich, Paul (1952). *The Courage to Be.* New Haven: Yale University Press.

2 Kierkegaard, Soren (1954). *Fear and Trembling and The Sickness Unto Death.* Garden City, NY: Doubleday.

3 Thomas, Dylan (1952). *The Poems of Dylan Thomas.* New York: New Directions.

4 Ferguson, Marilyn (1981). *The Aquarian Conspiracy.* Tarcher

5 Jong, Erica (1975). *Loveroot.* New York: Henry Holt & Company.

Copyright
Acknowledgements

I WISH TO THANK the copyright holders for permission to quote from the following poems and sources:

"Loving Arms," words and music by Tom Jans. Copyright © 1972 Almo Music Corp. (ASCAP). All Rights Reserved. International Copyright Secured.

"When I Loved Her" by Kris Kristofferson. © 1968 Careers-BMG Music Publishing, Inc. All Rights Reserved. Used by permission.

The Grapes of Wrath by John Steinbeck. Copyright 1939, renewed © 1967 by John Steinbeck. Used by permission of Viking Penguin, a division of Penguin Books USA Inc.

"A New Heaven and a New Earth," from *The Complete Poems of D.H. Lawrence* by D.H. Lawrence. Copyright © 1964, 1971 by Angelo Ravagli and C.M. Weekley, Executors of the Estate of Frieda Lawrence Ravagli. Used by permission of Viking Penguin, a division of Penguin Books USA Inc.

Excerpts from "The Downward Path to Wisdom" in *The Leaning Tower and Other Stories*, copyright 1939 and renewed 1969 by Katherine Anne Porter, reprinted by permission of Harcourt Brace Jovanovich, Inc.

"Lament" by Dylan Thomas, from *Poems of Dylan Thomas*. Copyright 1952 by Dylan Thomas. Reprinted by permission of New Directions Publishing Corporation.

"Testament (or Homage to Walt Whitman)" from *Loveroot* by Erica Jong. Copyright © 1968, 1969, 1973, 1974, 1975 by Erica Mann Jong. Reprinted by permission of Henry Holt and Company, Inc.

I and Thou, by Martin Buber, translated by Ronald Gregor Smith. Copyright © 1958 Charles Scribner's Sons; copyright renewed. Reprinted with permission of Charles Scribner's Sons, an imprint of Macmillan Publishing Company.

Awareness: Exploring, Experimenting, Experiencing, by John Stevens. © 1971 Real People Press. Reprinted by Permission.

"The Blue Unicorn" by Carol Mason. Copyright © Carol Mason. Reprinted by permission.

The Inner Game of Golf, by W. Timothy Gallwey. Copyright 1979, 1981, by W. Timothy Gallwey. Used by permission of Random House, Inc.